641.5964 H157f

LOS ALTOS

Hal, Fatema
The food of Morocco

33090004723286   LOSA

MAY 14 2003

W9-AMM-608

LONG BEACH PUBLIC LIBRARY
101 PACIFIC AVENUE
LONG BEACH, CA 90822

Published by Periplus Editions
with editorial offices at
130 Joo Seng Road #06-01
Singapore 368357

Copyright © 2002 Periplus Editions (HK) Ltd.

All rights reserved.

ISBN: 962-593-992-X

Library of Congress
Control Number: 2001096484

Publisher: Eric Oey
Associate Publisher: Christina Ong
Editors: Philip Tatham and Jocelyn Lau
Translator: Vincent Vichit-Vadakan
Production: Violet Wong and Chan Sow Yun

Photo credits
All food and location photography by Jean-François Hamon.
Additional photos by La Maison Arabe (Thierry Laureut),
p. 8; Magnum Photos (Bruno Barbey), pp. 2, 6–7, 10, 12,
14–15, 17, 19–21, 24–25, 26; and Valérie Millet, p. 22.

Acknowledgments
The publisher wishes to thank the following for their
generous assistance: Mr Ho Cheow Teck, Honorary
Consul, Consulate of the Kingdom of Morocco, Singapore;
Björn Conerding's, Ursula Haldimann, and Enija Luna of
Riad Enija; Mohamed Harda (hôtel Le Littoral), N'guyer
Hj Mustapha B. Hj Omar (Marrakesh), Liwan, Siècle,
Médina, Terre de Sable, Raynaud, Christofle, Baya,
Mokuba, Colline des Potiers, Fée d'Herbe ; Monette Aline,
Stéphanie Bertrand, Sandrine Duvillier, Joël Puentes,
Fabrizio Ruspoli (La Maison Arabe), and Samual Rodany.

Distributed by

USA
Tuttle Publishing
Airport Industrial Park
364 Innovation Drive
North Clarendon, VT 05759-9436
Tel: (802) 773-8930
Fax: (802) 773-6993

Japan
Tuttle Publishing
RK Building 2nd Floor
2-13-10 Shimo-Meguro, Meguro-Ku
Tokyo 153 0064, Japan
Tel: (81-3) 5437-0171
Fax: (81-3) 5437-0755

Asia Pacific
Berkeley Books Pte. Ltd.
130 Joo Seng Road #06-01
Singapore 368357
Tel: (65) 280-1330
Fax: (65) 280-6290

First Edition
Printed in Singapore

MAY 1 4 2003

THE FOOD OF
MOROCCO

Authentic Recipes from the North African Coast

Recipes and text by Fatema Hal
Photography by Jean-François Hamon and Bruno Barbey
Styling by Daniele Schnapp

PERIPLUS

3 3090 00472 3286

Contents

Part One: Food in Morocco

Moroccan cuisine has been nurtured by centuries of Mediterranean influence

The history of Morocco has always been closely intertwined with the history of the Mediterranean. As a veritable crossroads of civilizations—an asylum for the Andalousian Jews and Arabs who were chased out of the kingdom of Grenada at the end of the 15th century; later a French Protectorate until its independence in 1956—Morocco offers an exceptional example of generosity and harmony. This multifaceted country reflects diverse regional, ethnic, and social influences, all of which left their mark on its past. It is this variety that gives Moroccan cuisine its unparalleled reputation. Moroccan cuisine is considered to be one the finest in the world and some of its most celebrated dishes have justly taken their place among the culinary classics of the world.

The "Isle of the Sunset," Djerirat-al-Maghrib as the first Arab geographers named the land that would become Morocco, offers the traveler very diverse landscapes. First, there is the Atlantic Ocean lapping the shores in the west; then there are the Atlas and Rif Mountains that enclose a vast amphitheater reaching from the southwest to the northwest of Morocco; further south, the immense deserts that are still inhabited by nomadic peoples; and finally the central regions that spill out to the ocean where alternating plateaus, plains, and valleys have favored the development of culture and the rise of great cities.

The first inhabitants of Morocco were the Berbers who were invaded by the Omeyyad Arab dynasty of conquering warriors. Their empire reached from the Indus to the shores of northwest Africa. They built Muslim Spain and created a great civilization that reigned over the southern half of the peninsula and over Andalousia in particular.

In the eleventh and twelfth centuries, the Almoravid dynasty of Berbers, followed by the Almohad Berber dynasty, succeeded the Omeyyads as rulers of the Muslim territories in North Africa and Spain, and were responsible for the unification of Morocco.

Page 2:
The valley of Tinerhir, east of the High Atlas Mountains.
Opposite:
An impressive spread of tasty Moroccan snacks and appetizers.
Left:
Porters from Telouet carrying couscous and bread to a diffa *(banquet).*

The symbol of Marrakech and of Morocco as a whole, Jemaà el Fna Square bustles every evening with food stalls selling skewered meat, soups, snails, and much more. Jugglers, fire-eaters, snake charmers, storytellers, and monkey trainers add to the nightly spectacle.

found in every region of the kingdom but the recipes have been adapted to suit the conditions in which they are made.

Take couscous—the national dish—for example. In the countryside, the ruggedness of everyday life imposes a sense of humility in the preparation of the dish: dried fava (broad) beans replace garbanzo beans (chickpeas) while dried meat (*gueddid*) replaces the tenderer, subtler, and more expensive fresh lamb.

The coastal regions have developed their own original couscous called *kasksou baddaz*, in which dried sweet corn replaces the traditional semolina. In addition, fish from the Mediterranean or Atlantic enriches the dish.

Austere desert life also contributes its own touch. In the regions where man must often content himself with a few dates and a little milk, couscous is accompanied by small fresh dates (*kuran*) that are baked until almost candied. There are even varieties of couscous made from barley or rice, again reflecting the heritage of the *dadas*.

In the furthermost regions, meat is rare and dishes are invariably flavored with spices. Here, visual appearance is paramount. All the senses are called upon to appreciate these attractive dishes with their heady aromas. Cooks are as skilled in marrying tastes as they are in assembling colors.

Sub-Saharan Africa also left its mark on Morocco, trading its gold and other riches: the caravans that converged on the North included large numbers of women from Mali or the Sudan who would become the peerless *dadas*, the cooks who hold the secrets to the Moroccan kitchen.

It is this social and geographical diversity, and the peaceful cohabitation of different ethnic groups, that has enabled such a fine cuisine to evolve.

From north to south, Morocco offers travelers a wealth of contrasting landscapes. From the harsh winters of the Rif Mountains to the blazing caress of the Sahara, each region has developed its own ways with food, even if there are many elements that are shared from one province to the next. *Mechoui* (barbecued lamb) or *kessra* (bread) may be

The result is a cuisine that is festive and sensual. Some claim it even possesses medicinal qualities. Arab doctors have always made use of certain foods to cure their patients, without losing sight of the question of taste. One of them, Al-Rasi, hit upon the idea of coating medicinal decoctions in sugar to make the remedy more pleasant.

Religion has also played its part in shaping the eating habits of the Moroccan people. Religious directives addressed the issue of food early on and certain restrictions came into force. Pork is forbidden, as is any animal that has not been sacrificed in a religious rite—Jews refer to this sanctified meat as "kosher," Muslims call it "halal." Despite their solemnity, religious celebrations are also at the root of a number of original recipes that are served at specific times of the year. For example, it is with *harira* that the fast imposed by the month of Ramadan is broken every evening. This soup, both delicious and nourishing, soothes the hunger of the day and brings members of the family together. On these evenings, and much to the delight of the children present, pastries such as *grioch*, *shebbakiya*, *selou*, and *sfenji* are also served.

It is in the great imperial cities that the Moroccan *art de vivre* reaches its zenith. Note the words of a civil servant from the finance ministry in 1885: "Thus at last, Great Chamberlain, will the preparations to welcome the Sultan be concluded. No fewer than thirty-three dishes will follow: salads, couscous, *pastilla*, *tagine* of poultry, meat, fish [...]. Scoundrels from backwater provinces will be left speechless before such abundance and magnificence and they will admire with near religious devotion the white bread served for the occasion."

Large meals, or *diffa*, follow an immutable ritual: salads are served one after the other and then make way for the famous *pastilla* (pie) of pigeon. This is followed by *mechoui* (barbecued lamb), various *tagine* (stewed dishes), the couscous, and, finally, mouthwatering pastries.

A flask of scented water is always passed among guests so they may wash their hands and rinse their palates. Finally, guests enjoy a glass of mint tea, the gratifying conclusion to any great *diffa* worthy of the name.

Opening the doors to Morocco, we enter a world of tastes and colors that reveal great richness and incomparable skills. In doing so, we perpetuate an authentic tradition, a refined and unequaled celebration of the senses.

This shop in the Aït Ourir souk (market) east of Marrakech offers tagines cooked over kanounes, a kind of clay cauldron.

The Riches of a Generous Past

*Morocco's sumptuous history of cooking has placed
the country on the world's culinary stage*

History has rarely provided a better example of people living in such effortless communion than medieval Andalousia. Back then, Christians, Jews, and Muslims shared the same lands and the same way of life. Each group developed its own faith, and art rose to the heights of grace. O blessed Andalousia, for a time the Mediterranean blew a wind of peace onto your shores. But at the end of the fifteenth century, this peace was irrevocably shattered when the Catholic kings from the north broke the truce and forced the Jews and Muslims to choose between conversion or exile.

Banished from Spain, some took refuge in North Africa, perpetuating their long tradition of peaceful cohabitation. Their food, music, and dress were very similar. Admitedly, in the kasbah of Algiers or in the alleyways of Marrakech, the Jews had separate quarters reserved for them, but everyone lived together on good terms. With their shared history, it is difficult today to unravel the bonds that unite Jews and Muslims. As a reflection of this history, Moroccan cuisine is a veritable lesson in sharing, curiosity, generosity, and harmony.

The regional cuisine of the Berbers was already in existence when the Muslim Arabs arrived. Later, the *dadas* (female slaves) from Bilad Al-Sudan and the Jews who were banished from Spain each, in turn, enriched the culinary art of Morocco. Despite them living in close quarters and accumulating culinary skills, many dishes retained their uniqueness.

I remember that my mother adored eating *rkak* (*matzo*, unleavened bread) that our Jewish neighbor made. Whenever our neighbor could, she would give some to my mother, who would offer her own homemade bread in return. As they enjoyed each other's breads, they traded their baking secrets. But since neither was ever completely successful in making the other's recipe, they continued to exchange their breads as they had before. Our table was rich and varied with Jewish cuisine distinguishing itself through its pastries and the subtlety of its breads.

Unlike in other regions where Ottoman occupation resulted in the disappearance of local culinary traditions, Moroccan cooking was gently imbued with the influences of foreign cuisines. The exiles who arrived from Grenada were warmly welcomed and, in the same vein, African slaves from the south were generally well treated.

The dining room of a traditional restaurant looking onto a patio planted with orange trees.

No border is impenetrable. At the northeastern tip of Morocco, the town of Oujda faces that of Tlemcen, in Algeria. For centuries, travelers crossed the border in both directions carrying with them their foods and culinary skills—their invisible heritage—thus rendering the exact origins of many dishes impossible to determine.

Despite the difficulties in tracing the culinary history of Morocco, there is one unwavering fact: only the cooking of the ancient communities has found a place and made a lasting impression among the peoples it encountered. In the nineteenth century, Europeans imported new utensils and products but their influence is only very recent because, as it must be remembered, their interaction with the locals was limited to purely administrative affairs.

In an Algerian novel, a *fellah* (or farmhand) recalls how he had never seen sugar as white as that brought by American soldiers during World War II. At the time, such a product was only available on the black market. It was only in the 1970s that French cuisine took hold here, with *hors d'œuvres*, sweets, and remarkable pastries. The bakeries that made round bread saw production drop in favor of carefully calibrated baguettes. Even

A Berber shepherd leads his flock through the Aït Bouguemez Valley in the High Atlas Mountains, where most of the country's sheep and goat livestock come from.

the *sfenjis*—fritters sold on the streets which children delighted in—have been supplanted.

As in many countries where cooking benefits from the privilege of tradition, good restaurants are rare in Morocco. If a traveler is not invited to the table in a private home, he will leave with an indifferent impression of Moroccan cuisine. Large hotels prefer to serve indefinable international cuisine to please the masses, rather than offer traditional fare that might upset the undiscriminating tourist. And that is how the gourmet could miss the roads that lead to the delicate flavors of a pigeon *pastilla* or a patiently simmered *tagine* of apricots and pine nuts. Unless, that is, he meets a Moroccan family who will take it upon themselves to defend the culinary honor of their country.

For Moroccan cuisine is in fact family cooking. It demands the communion of family members for the traditional dinner at home or, less frequently, for a wedding, a birth, or a baptism. Each family adds its own personal touch, some jealously guarded secret only handed down from mother to daughter. The art requires both skill and memory. Most older Moroccan women are not familiar with the written word. Morocco belongs to a civilization where giving one's word is worth more than a piece of paper, where speaking is a surer signature than can be made with the ink of a pen.

So we run the risk of seeing dishes that formerly enjoyed widespread admiration disappear. Tastes change, as do methods of cooking and conservation. Time works faster than a thoroughbred from the royal stables; the *dadas* are disappearing, and with them, their vast culinary knowledge.

The dominant roles played by Europe and the United States in today's world arena greatly influences the way of life in the other continents. If traditional Moroccan fare is not often found in restaurants in Morocco, it is because when Moroccans go out today, they are seeking food that is new and different.

Today, rice is part of the diet in many Moroccan households, and ketchup and Coca-Cola also have their place on the kitchen table. In some places, *pastilla* is even garnished with Chinese noodles!

It is pointless to remain closed to all foreign influences—an impossible feat anyway in the face of the unstoppable progression of globalization—but changes should be made with respect for the balance of a dish to prevent it becoming an ungainly amalgam of incompatible parts.

Out of respect for bread, it must not be touched by a knife, which would be considered an act of violence. Bread should be broken. Food that has been given by God and blessed in His name before the meal should not be degraded by such an instrument.

Apart from a few notable exceptions, it is comparatively difficult to find a large number of good Moroccan restaurants within the country. Paradoxically, the situation is quite different abroad. In the United States, France, Britain, and throughout the world, there are many excellent eateries that, for the most part, respect the Moroccan culinary traditions. Moroccan cuisine is, without doubt, a good export.

However, it would be a mistake to claim that one must travel outside Morocco to enjoy traditional Moroccan food. The Moroccans are noted for their hospitality, so do accept all invitations to visit Moroccan homes, join the inhabitants at their kitchen tables, and share in their simple, subtle, and very tasty recipes.

Women and Dadas

Moroccan cuisine is essentially a feminine art

In Morocco, cuisine is first and foremost women's business. In Moroccan culture, men are strongly advised to stay away from ovens, or risk losing their virility.

Morocco is a country of oral tradition, even though progress and education are gradually reaching across the immense territory. Here, knowledge, culinary or otherwise, is dispensed by word of mouth, from mother to daughter. So, should you be invited into a Moroccan home and the mistress of the house allows you free reign after the indispensable mint tea ceremony, you will not see any books on the subject of food and you will certainly not find any recipe books.

We have seen that Morocco is rich in its varied populations. The Berbers were the first inhabitants. Several ethnological studies have shown that Berber women worked the land, harvested, picked, and did the cooking themselves. Clearly our culinary roots go back to cultures from pre-Islamic times (North Africa

was the larder of the Roman Empire) and can be traced to local *savoir faire*. Since that time, Morocco has had close commercial ties with countries in the south of the continent; sub-Saharan Africa provided gold, salt, and slaves. Trade reached its height under the green banner of Islam and became a flourishing commerce that affected the whole society including the cuisine.

Brutal import of servant populations was quickly replaced by peaceful solutions, and it was usually through trade that abundant supplies of slaves were sent to the market of Dâr al-Islam, the house of Islam. In Morocco, male and female slaves came primarily from Sudan. Many had been bought by Touareg traders for a few pieces of gold and some scraps of fabric; others had simply been rounded up on the banks of the Niger. They instructed the captives in the rudiments of Arabic and the principles of Islam (which increased their market value) before leading them to Moroccan markets where they were sold.

Opposite:
The great tradition of street food is perpetuated by the women of Morocco.
Left:
Desert-dwelling nomad women prepare couscous, the national dish of Morocco.

We do not know much about the living conditions of the first sub-Saharan African slaves. Observers conclude that, at least after the nineteenth century, they did not suffer at the hands of their employers. The masters even tended to be more humane with sub-Saharan African slaves because though originally pagan, they quickly chose to convert to Islam.

Female slaves, known as *dadas,* quickly became indispensable, and were even given the charge of young children, for whom their *dadas* remain an indelible memory. Bound to slavery during the lifetime of their masters, some of the *dadas* stayed on in the house of the heirs when the latter died, to continue doing what they did as slaves, though henceforth as free women.

Right:
Mouloud, *one of the most important Muslim holidays, celebrates the birth of the prophet Mohammed. It is marked by processions, dancing, and feasts.*
Opposite:
Until recently, women were kept away from the classroom so they derived their power from cooking.

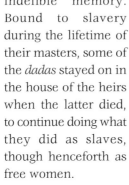

Almost all female slaves were destined to perform domestic tasks. However, through the attention of a merchant or a rich master, a few, thought to be good learners, received a thorough education in music or even literature, before being sent to the harems of many an Orientalist's fancy.

Qualified cooks were sold for very large sums. Restrictive and strict regulations were set so that the cooks' instruction conformed to the wishes of the palace. Over the course of several years, the cooks were fed, housed, and trained until they perfected their knowledge and skill. The training period was crowned by a sort of diploma, a certificate with the slave's name and her culinary aptitudes. It comes as no surprise that these slaves commanded such high prices.

Other than the original contributions from Berber culture, Moroccan cuisine is largely made up of the heritage of the *dadas* whose numbers are now dwindling. The height of irony is that these women whose only wealth was their status as a slave have become the masters of an inestimable, delectable treasure. When a *dada* is no more, a whole chapter of our culinary heritage is lost. To borrow the words of African writer Hampaté Bâ: "When one of them passes away, it is a library burning." It has become urgent to record all the recipes and kitchen hints of these women in order to preserve their memories, which have been jealously guarded in household kitchens.

Heiresses to an ancient knowledge, these women have acquired real power in the home. It has been one of the only means at their disposal to demonstrate their competence and the hours they have spent tending their ovens may soon be lost forever, as will a part of our culinary memory.

Grand Imperial Cuisine

*The art and splendor of Moroccan cooking is in the fabled cities
of Rabat, Fes, Meknes, and Marrakech.*

Right:
Tanjia
marrakshia *is
a dish made by
men for men.
This meat dish
takes the name
of the* tanjia,
*or eartherware
amphora, in
which it is cooked.
Sealed with paper
and string, the
amphora is
baked for as long
as four hours.*
Opposite:
Riads *are elegant
homes discreetly
nestled in the
heart of medinas,
which house a
central patio
decorated with
a fountain.*

Since the seventeenth century, no fewer than four imperial cities have laid claim to being the capital of the sherifan empire of Morocco. Rabat, Fes, Meknes, and Marrakech are all names that ring out as splendors of the past. Each was the capital in its time and they have never ceased being rivals. All have laid claim to their own styles of architecture, music and, of course, cooking.

Marrakech was founded in the eleventh century by Berber horsemen from southern Morocco, under the leadership of Youssef Ibn Tachfine who established the Almoravid dynasty, before being conquered by the Almohad sultan Abd al-Mumin in AD 1147. The city first owed its fame to the fact that it was on the trade route from Timbuktu to the north, used by caravans laden with spices and gold coins. Today, the cuisine of Marrakech is notably rich and is a reminder of those luxurious times of old. It is a somewhat ostentatious fare that is presented to foreigners who flow through the gates of city.

The *souks* (markets) are unforgettable. They are

bursting with spices and you can still purchase real *ras el hanout*, the fabulous alchemy of twenty-seven spices that is almost impossible to find today. It is also the city of *tanjia marrakshia*, a dish initially served only to unmarried men, which has gradually become the symbol of the local cuisine. There is also chicken with nigella seeds, couscous with sumach, and *mezgueldi*, a *tagine* of lamb with caramelized onions. Add to the delights of the palate vestiges from the past. Visit the Koutoubia mosque, the beacon of Almohad art, the famed square Jemaà el Fna, the koranic school Medersa Ben Youssef, the gardens of Menara, and the old medina.

Fes, founded by Moulay Idriss, was the refuge for Muslims and Jews who were forced out of Andalousia beginning in the ninth century. The last refugees arrived in the labyrinthine city in AD 1492, as the final tears fell on the cheeks of the last sultan of Grenada, Boabdil, who was defeated by the Catholic kings. Fes el Jedid, a living *mélange* of cultures, was declared capital of the empire in AD 1250. In the dazzling

homes that conceal their beauty behind the high walls of the old city of Fes, refined dishes are presented with style and grace. The cuisine of Fes resembles that of Tlemcen, a shared heritage from Andalousia of which both cities are proud. Fes has its lamb and squash *tagine* with honey; its vermicelli couscous with pigeons; its various recipes for carrots, savory, sweet or with cumin; its pigeon *pastilla*; and its partridge couscous. A must-see is the Karaouiyine mosque, the most prestigious Arab Muslim university of the medieval world, built to the glory of Allah in the ninth century, where precious manuscripts from the libraries of Grenada, Seville, and Cordoba found refuge after Spain fell to the Reconquista. Don't miss the Danan synagogue, built in the seventeenth century in the *mellah*, the Jewish quarter, or the marvelous *souk* (market).

Meknes, the former capital of Moulay Ismaël, the Alawite sovereign, is the least well-known of the four imperial cities as a tourist destination. Modest in size, Meknes has retained the languor that is customary in provincial cities. In a city with a large Jewish population, tolerance reigns. And the cuisine is a conscious reflection of this openness. If it is true that the Jewish community has its own recipes, like chicken pâté, potato *pastilla* or stuffed mutton intestine, Muslims were also proud of their own cuisine that was similar to that of nearby Fes. But inhabitants of Meknes are supposedly stingy with their wealth and it is no accident that one of their specialties is called "the hen has flown." Guests are promised a dish of chicken and garbanzo beans but what a surprise to see plates served only with beans! When the host is asked where the meat is, he invariably replies that the hen has flown off.

Rabat, the modern capital, has attracted many guests to its table. If the bazaars are not as showy as those of Fes or Marrakech, it is because the city prefers calm and modernity. Here reigns the cuisine of the *makhzen*, the official cuisine that has ties to every region of Morocco and the neighboring countries. Home cooking, rich and varied, is in every way astonishing. Some recipes are carefully guarded secrets like the famous *bal farkh* couscous made with sea bass.

A coastal city, Rabat shares the secrets of the sea with the other coastal towns of Assafi and Essaouira, but Rabat has no equal when it comes to cooking shad, a fish similar to the sardine. Assafi and Essaouira are famous for serving *baddaz*, couscous made from sweet corn, garnished with conger eel heads, and fried moray eal with honey.

In Rabat, you will also find *kaak*, a delicious cake, or *zemata*, a dish made with seeds (in Oujda, the town on the Algerian border, it is made with young wheat and covered with figs.)

Although the city of Tetouan is not strictly speaking an imperial city, its history renders it indispensable. In its vast memory reside the splendors of Muslim Andalousia, its riches, and its subtle perfumes. A direct heir to the culinary traditions of Grenada, Teotouan is also one of the only Moroccan cities to have been subjected to the influence of the Ottomans as the presence of *bakhlava* and *ktaifs* attests, giving a special accent to border and coastal towns. We should also mention the *pastilla* of chicken with preserved lemons.

A fountain in an old residence in Fes.

Food and Religion

Abstinence and culinary feasts
in honor of Islam

An active member of the Islamic community, or *umma*, Morocco proudly proclaims its religious heritage. The king, in addition to his role as chief executive, is also the spiritual guide for his subjects. The Alowite dynasty, from which both the King of Morocco and the King of Jordan are descended, is one of the branches that traces its roots directly back to the prophet Mohammed. Religion is very present in the hearts of all Moroccans.

In the words of a nineteenth century French traveler, Eugène Fromentin, as taken from his journal published in AD 1857 as *A Summer in the Sahara*, to understand that food and the divine form a whole in Morocco, "you must see that in Arab beliefs eating and giving something to eat are solemn acts and that a *diffa* (feast) is a great lesson in *savoir vivre*, generosity, and sharing attentions. Take note that it is not due to any social obligations…but in virtue of a divine inspiration, and, to use their words, it is as a messenger from God that the traveler is welcomed by his host. Their politeness therefore is explained not by conventions but rather is based on religious principle. They practice it with the same respect they have for all things that are holy and do so as an act of devotion. Therefore it is not at all a laughing matter to see robust men, in warrior's attire with their amulets round their necks, stoically performing the small household duties that in Europe fall to women; seeing their large hands, hardened by the handling of horses and the practice of arms, serving at the table, slicing meat before serving it to you, showing the best cut in the back of a mutton, holding the carafe or, between each course, offering serviettes made of handwoven wool. These attentions, which in our world appear puerile, perhaps even ridiculous, here become touching because of the contrast that exists between the man and the humble tasks he performs with strength and dignity.

Celebrations such as family visits, weddings, and circumcisions are all occasions for the lady of the house to show off her culinary talents.

Opposite:
At a royal wedding, a procession accompanied by musicians bears the gifts for the future spouse.

Left:
In large cities, every neighborhood has one or more public bread ovens where you can leave your bread, and even your cakes or mechoui (barbecued lamb), to be cooked.

Likewise, for religious holidays such as the Prophet's birthday, Laylat al Qadr, Laylat al Seghir, Ashoura, and the month of Ramadan, daily fares give way to festive and culinary celebrations.

Among the Five Pillars of Islam, Ramadan holds a special place. The Prophet wanted this to test the faith of the converts, and fasting lasts 30 days. It is a way of bringing families together to share the food that will deliver the soul at sunset.

In the medina, when the baker lights his ovens, loaves are brought on large platters or boards. To distinguish one loaf of bread from another, specially designed stamps or fingerprints are made in the dough.

Unlike Christian fasting which is considered penitence, atonement for sins, and a battle against natural instincts, fasting during Ramadan is for a Muslim a way to serve God, to pay homage to Him. Thus Ramadan has become a period of joy, and pride for the believer who is given the opportunity to manifest his belonging to Islam. It is a period of celebration that is given concrete expression around the table in the form of delicious foods.

From the time Muslims get up, they must avoid any transgression; not the merest drop of coffee must taint their empty cup. And because nothing is as present as what is absent, mothers outdo themselves during the sacred month to produce all their culinary dreams both savory, and especially sweet. Everything is timed and planned. People are purified and pray, they pardon, they enter the kitchen more often than usual in an effort to trick their hunger. It is a wonderful month, where days extend into the languorous night. Muslims live at night and sleep in the morning. Women create, invent, or reproduce old recipes. Men, unable to go to the café, fill the streets, the mosques, and the markets, which become more colorful than usual. At night, there is a ballet of dishes and sweets, but the queen of the month is *harira*. Dates too are served. Is it not said that the Prophet himself broke his fast with dates and milk? Round tables, tablecloths, earthenware and porcelain bowls, glasses of milk, dates, *shebakiya*...he who has not visited a Moroccan house at this time has seen nothing, smelled nothing. Never are so many scents, colors, and desires brought together as they are for Ramadan.

After breaking the fast each evening, contented believers throng the alleyways. Nothing is better than a full stomach. Then comes *iisha*, the dinner hour and time for the last prayer, and for a second time we go back to the table: meat and poultry, asparagus with eggs, fruits, salads, and of course sweets of all kinds: *grioush*, *zalabiya*, *halwat tourk*, Turkish *halva*, gazelle horns from Fes, and *makrout* from Tlemcen.

Then comes the twenty-seventh day. The day of days that announces the Night of Destiny (or Night of Power) during which anything can happen. It is said that the Prophet Mohammed received his first revelation in the last ten days of the month of Ramadan, and the *ulamas* (religious leaders) decided to end the event on the twenty-seventh day of the month. Since that time, a lamb has been sacrificed by the richest families, a chicken by the less well-to-do, and couscous is prepared for the mosque where it will be distributed to the least fortunate. In the last few years, it would seem that due to a resurgence of faith, prayers last until dawn. Then comes Laylet al Seghir. All the children wear new clothes. Everywhere houses are filled with cakes made during the last week of Ramadan. Neighbors and cousins meet to blanch and skin almonds or to steam dates. Dozens and dozens of eggs are broken, sesame seeds toasted, anise seeds ground. Everybody participates to give the festivities a special air.

Each family rivals the next with inventions. One will ask a cousin from Algeria or another from a different region of Morocco for a recipe unknown in these parts. On the morning of Laylet al Seghir, all the aromas regain their rightful place after a month of absence: the boiling coffee flows once again in the glasses and white cups.

Among the other principles of the Koran, there are restrictions that everyone must obey. Pork meat is deemed to be illicit, as is any animal that has not been bled. An animal is not slaughtered, it is sacrificed. Blood renders flesh impure. If an animal has not been bled in accordance with religious law, then it is carrion (*djifa*) and banned.

This rule also applies to game. All wild animals that are not specifically banned by the Holy Book may be eaten. When one wants to kill animals whose flesh can be eaten, one must turn to face the East and cut its throat while saying "Allahu Akbar!" (God is great). Where animals that live in water are concerned, the doctrines differ, depending on the various rites. Some allow the eating of all such animals, but others have exceptions—frogs, in particular, are the subject of much debate. On the other hand, cricket flesh is legal, as long as it is captured alive and killed by a Muslim. It is said that the Prophet's wives considered it to be a delicacy. The most sacred food in Morocco is bread. Given by God, it is the food most surrounded by tradition. If a Muslim Moroccan finds a piece of bread on the ground, tradition dictates that he pick it up, kiss it, and place it somewhere where it will not be soiled.

Street food is a Moroccan tradition. There are the classic dishes and there are the masters who prepare them. Here is a mechoui (barbecued lamb) "specialist" from Marrakech.

Moroccan Hospitality

*An invitation into the home
is always celebrated with a serving of tea*

Whether very poor or incredibly rich, Moroccans all share a truly exceptional sense of hospitality. It is not unusual to see that a friend of the family is often better looked after than the family's own son. The guest, treated with respect and honored with an engaging smile, must never under any circumstances refuse what he is offered or he risks bringing shame on his hosts. Hospitality is so sacred that members of the family will bend over backwards to accommodate a visiting friend.

It must be said that in Morocco, as in most Arab and Muslim countries, the whole family comes together for meals, men in one room, women in another, though this practice is quickly losing ground in the urban centers of Casablanca and Rabat. At mealtimes, each diner takes his or her place around a low table upon which the couscous or the *tagine* is served from a common dish, and nimbly uses thumb, index, and middle fingers of the right hand to serve himself a piece of meat or a little semolina.

Regardless of the setting, even in this carpet bazaar, tea is likely to accompany any discussion in Morocco.

The symbolism associated with bread is very strong. If someone tries to share a piece of bread that has been given him with another guest at the table, it may be thought that he is looking for a fight with the person who originally served the bread to him.

Traditional clay *tagine* pots are slowly disappearing from the Moroccan table in response to changing tastes. Today it is not surprising to see a Chinese serving dish on an embroidered Berber tablecloth.

The tea ceremony remains a special moment when entertaining guests. Even though it is a relatively recent practice—it was probably introduced in the eighteenth or nineteenth centuries—tea is particularly valued and has quickly become one of the most powerful symbols of the Moroccan kingdom.

"The whole universe is found in a teapot," writes Abdallah Zrika. "Or more accurately, the *sinia* (circular platter) represents the earth, the teapot the heavens, and the glasses rain; the heavens by way of the rain is joined to the earth."

At first reserved only for the very wealthy because of its exorbitant cost, the consumption of tea quickly became widespread. In the palaces of Marrakech, on the slopes of the Atlas Mountains or in the blazing heat of a nomad's tent, the infusion remains the drink favored by all Moroccans. Tea invariably concludes a meal and figures in discussions at any sidewalk café. It is served at breakfast, during the morning break, after lunch, as an apéritif, and after dinner. It is present at every hour of a Moroccan's day.

Preparing and serving the drink is a true art. A layer of tea is placed in glimmering teapots, followed by fresh mint leaves, broken lumps of sugar, and boiling water. Sometimes absinthe leaves are added to give the tea a slightly bitter edge. The host takes the teapot and pours the precious drink into a small glass from as high as he can. The contents are then poured back into the teapot and the pouring repeated until the mint, tea, and sugar are perfectly combined. Only then does the satisfied host hand each guest a steaming glass of tea.

Great feasts, diffa, always end with a firework display of pastries, served with mint tea.

All Roads Lead to the Souk

A festival of colors and
a triumph of the senses

Every Moroccan city harbors a medina, the old quarter where the past still echoes clearly and the flow of passers-by is never-ending. Here are found the craftsmen, the traders, and the gossip that will be the subject of lively discussions in the *hammam*, or traditional steam baths.

A treasure trove worthy of Ali Baba, and guarded by massive gates, the *souk* is a succession of narrow, often covered, alleyways, with back-to-back shops that are barely bigger than a linen cupboard. Tinsmiths, grocers, butchers, pastry chefs, tailors, spice merchants, and cake vendors meet daily and co-exist in indescribable mayhem.

If Moroccan cuisine enjoys such prestige, it is because it has, over the centuries, learned to refine its judgment and satisfy the demands of the palate, the eyes, and the nose as few cuisines have. If, as we have already mentioned, Arab doctors used spices very early on in their remedies, they also knew how to give their patients a sense of taste for finer things. Spices play an important role in their remedies, and are used in preparing the most astonishing recipes. In a society in which restrictions abound, there exists a whole range of local remedies that have a powerful following—from love potions to cures for sterility, spices hold the answer to all our everyday woes. Grandmothers'

recipes live long in Morocco. In the home, women often deploy their imagination, ingenuity, and skill to stay in good health. Swallowing two spoonfuls of cumin to counter stomach flu requires a little bravery. But does it matter, if these little tricks heal the body and ease the mind?

Morocco is the birth place of the rare and surprising *ras el hanout*, "head of the shop" in Arabic, the heady mixture of twenty-seven spices, the secret of which is jealously guarded in the memories of a handful of shopkeepers in the dark alleys of the *souks* in Fes and Marrakech.

In the *souk*, the merchant, perched atop his colorful displays, calls to the passer-by. Drunken on the spell of words and smells, transfixed by the shimmering colors, the shopper purchases caraway seeds, cloves, nigella seeds, cinnamon, mace, and cumin in little folded bags. Once home, the man hands his wife the precious sachets with which she will prepare the dishes for the next meal.

The odors, flavors, and scents play an important role in Morocco. They are synonymous with gates that lead to the sublime. In every home, hidden in small containers or old battered tins, are the spices that give Moroccan cuisine a touch of color and exude their delicate perfume.

In the souk, different activities are located in different quarters: the baboush (Moroccan slippers) souk, the henna souk, the souk of the luthiers, the copperware souk, and the vegetable market.

Part Two: Cooking in Morocco

*A variety of traditional and modern cooking utensils
are found in Moroccan kitchens today*

One of the most important kitchen utensils is the **tagine**. The term *tagine* describes both the food—a long-cooked stew, usually of lamb or chicken—and the earthenware cooking recipient in which it is cooked. A *tagine* has a round, shallow base and a tall, pointed cover and *tagine* dishes are prepared by long simmering over an open fire or a bed of charcoal.

A **tanjia** describes both the food and the earthenware amphora that is used to cook the specialty of Marrakech, *tanjia marrakshia*. The amphora containing the meat and spices is simply sealed with paper and string and baked for several hours.

Couscous, the staple food of Morocco, resembles tiny balls of dough which are steamed and served like rice, often mixed with a *tagine* stew. The balls of dough are made not by kneading but by sprinkling salted water into a **gasaa**—a large dish once made of clay or wood but today mostly available in stainless steel or aluminum—containing flour (from wheat, barley, or maize) while the fingers of the right hand are slowly raked through the flour causing the dough to form tiny balls which are then dried. (A *gasaa* is also used to knead dough for bread.) Couscous is steamed in a **quadra wa alkaskas**, or

Ghorbal

couscoussier, which has two parts: the lower part for cooking the vegetables and the meat or fish, and the top—which has a perforated bottom—for steaming the couscous.

Indispensable for serving mint tea is the **l'barrade**, a tin, sliver plate, or stainless steel teapot. Other traditional kitchen utensils that are still seen today include the **ghorbal**, or sieve made from pierced leather, and the **chtato**,

Couscoussier

or silk-lined sieve. Cooking pots and pans include the **maqla**, or copper skillet, the **quarda** and **tanjir**, different kinds of large copper stewing pots, and the **tanjra** which was originally a clay pot although today, the stainless steel version is more widely used.

Tagines

Cooking Methods

Mastering a few traditional cooking methods is both simple and rewarding

THREE STEPS TO COOKING COUSCOUS

Couscous is the name given to both the cooked dish and the semolina. A staple food of much of North Africa, couscous is now very popular in Europe and North America. Many brands of couscous are marked "instant" and offer instructions for cooking in the microwave or oven. If you don't wish to follow these instructions, you are encouraged to try the traditional Moroccan way of preparing couscous which is easily mastered. All you need to watch for is the steam escaping from the couscoussier. Cooking couscous occurs in three stages:
• About 45 minutes before you want to eat, wet 1 lb (500 g) couscous with a little water in a *gasaa*, or large dish. Every grain must be moistened so that it can expand when cooked. Place the couscous in the basket of the couscoussier. Cover the rim of the lower half of the couscoussier with foil to form a seal so that the steam will not escape from the sides.

Place the basket part of the couscoussier over the simmering sauce in which the meat and vegetables are cooking. Cover and steam for 30 minutes, ensuring that the steam is going through the couscous.
• Pour the couscous, now a compact mass, into the *gasaa*, or large dish. Using a fork or a slotted spoon, break up the "cake" that has formed, adding a little cold water to help break up the lumps. Add salt to taste. Return the couscous to the steam basket over the stock, cover and wait for the steam to rise through the grains.
• The couscous is almost ready. Pour it back into the *gasaa*, or large dish, one last time. Take a generous piece of butter and mix it into the couscous to separate each grain. Return the semolina to the steamer and remove from heat as soon as the steam penetrates the couscous. Serve hot in a shallow dish. Arrange couscous in a dome and place vegetables and meat around the couscous. Serve the broth separately.

MAKING SMEN

Being a Berber tradition, *smen*, or salted butter, is unique to the area. The butter is first clarified—it is melted and the solids are removed—then sometimes simmered with herbs, strained, and salt added. *Smen* is often buried and aged until it is very pungent. This recipes is easier to prepare and is more acceptable to non-Maghribi palates.

1 teaspoon large-grain semolina
2 cups (400 g) butter
2 teaspoons salt

In a heavy saucepan, cook the semolina and the butter over very low heat for 5 minutes, stirring regularly. Filter through a fine sieve and add salt. Mix thoroughly. Pour into an earthenware bowl and leave to cool. *Smen* will keep for up to one year.

MAKING WAARKA

9 cups (1 kg) all-purpose (plain) flour
Pinch salt
1 tablespoon olive oil
4 cups (1 liter) lukewarm water

Mix the flour, salt, and oil, then gradually add the water, kneading to obtain a soft, elastic dough. Place the dough in a bowl, sprinkle with a little water, cover and leave to rest for about 1 hour.

Boil water in a pot covered with a smooth, flat copper pan or a non-stick baking sheet. When the metal is hot, reduce heat. In the past, the metal was rubbed with an onion dipped in egg yolk to prevent the dough from sticking.

Take a handful of dough. With a regular movement of the wrist, quickly touch the lump of dough to the griddle. When the dough touches the metal, it will leave a thin round film on the metal. Repeat quickly several times, leaving no gaps between each touch, in order to form a large, almost transparent sheet. Remove very carefully and keep prepared sheets under a damp cloth until ready to use.

This requires a bit of dexterity so, if you don't have neither the time, buy ready-made filo pastry instead.

FOLDING BRIWATTES

Cut the sheets of *waarka* into strips, place a spoonful of filling at one end, fold the corner over at a right angle, then continue folding at right angles. Tuck in the last edge as you would an envelope (see photos below).

Moroccan Ingredients

Morocco,
land of spices and herbs

Cinnamon

Cloves

Cumin

ABSINTHE: This silver-colored plant can be added to mint or can replace it during the winter. It reinforces the taste of mint and brings out the taste of tea with a slight bitter aftertaste. Omit if not available.

ANISEED (*naaffaa de tafilalte*): The translation of the Arabic name of this spice is "that which does good." It flavors our pastries but also certain dishes like Chicken with Anise.

CARAWAY SEEDS (*kerouya de meknes*): Similar to cumin in appearance, but very different in taste. This spice is most often used in preparing certain salads, and especially in *harira*, the famed Moroccan soup.

CHILI (*felfla harra*): Although used in everyday cooking, chilies are practically banned from festive tables.

CILANTRO (*kosbore*): Cilanto, or fresh coriander leaf, is often used with flat leaf parsley to season fish and poultry.

CINNAMON (*farfa*): Widely used in Moroccan cuisine. Used in sticks or ground, this seductive spice can be smooth or violent—it is up to you to add the right amount!

CLOVES (*oud ennouar*): The Arabic translation is "wood of flower." Moroccan cooks use it in savory dishes, soups, and pastries.

CUBEB (*el kebaba*): This is my favorite spice. Also known as tailed pepper or Java pepper, cubeb is native to Indonesia and was introduced to Arabic cooking as early as the tenth century. Cubeb resembles black peppercorns with a little stalk or "tail" protruding from one end. Its taste is subtle, between nutmeg and cloves. Cubeb is used in savory dishes and in pastries like *markouts*, little diamonds of semolina with honey and dates.

CUMIN: Ground cumin should be used sparingly because it can enliven the taste of fish, for example, or it can kill all its flavor. It is often used with carrots, fava beans (board beans), and *kefta* (ground meat). Cumin can also be used whole (*camoune hab*).

FENUGREEK (*l'halba*): These small yellow grains have a very intense flavour. Use sparingly to preserve the balance of a dish, not to make it unbearably bitter.

GINGER (*sekine jbire*): It is often used in dry powder form in Morocco. Ginger is also considered to be an aphrodisiac. Wisdom dictates using it carefully, or running the danger of making a dish bitter.

HARISSA: A hot, red paste of chili and other herbs and spices popular in Morocco and North Africa. It is often made at home by blending red chilies with such ingredients as caraway, coriander, salt, and oil to form a paste but it is also readily available in cans from most North African and Arab groceries.

KHLI': A kind of preserved meat which is sold in jars and is available from Moroccan and other Arab groceries.

LAFT EL MAHFOUR: A very strong flavored turnip, with a slight bitter aftertaste, used in making *tagines* and couscous.

MARJORAM (*merdedouche*): Walking through the streets of a Moroccan town, who could fail to notice the immense pans filled with snail soup? It is primarily seasoned with marjoram.

MALLOW (*bakoula khoubiz*): Mallow is our spinach. It grows everywhere. Steamed and seasoned with paprika and cumin, it is present on all Moroccan tables.

MASTIC or GUM ARABIC: Subtly flavored, it is used in pigeon *pastilla*.

MINT (*na'na*): It is unthinkable to end a meal without mint tea. This herb has one of the most striking flavors in Morocco.

NIGELLA SEEDS: These little black seeds (also called black onion seeds), which are so full of flavor, are grown in Morocco. They are often found on bread, but also in certain *tagines*, like the *Tagine* of Chicken in Nigella Seeds.

NUTMEG (*el gouza*): A "strong" spice, it is only rarely used. Whole nutmegs keep almost indefinitely.

PARSLEY (*maadnous*): Flat leaf parsley is used in almost all Moroccan dishes. It is indispensable for the *shermoula* (a mixture of herb and spice).

PEPPER (*l'bazare*): Both black and white pepper is used in the Moroccan kitchen with freshly ground black pepper slightly more in evidence.

RAS EL HANOUT: A finely balanced composition of twenty-seven spices, the secret of which is closely guarded within the walls of a few select *souk* (markets). *Ras el hanout* blends, cardamom, mace, galangal, grains of paradise, the fruit, and the nut of nutmeg, allspice, Spanish fly, cinnamon and Chinese cinnamon, long pepper, white and black pepper, cloves, tumeric, ginger and white ginger, lavender, iris, rose buds, nigella, belladonna berries, ash tree nuts, *gouza el asnab*, *hil al abachi* (the fruit of a perennial shrub), and chasteberry.

SAFFRON (*zaafrane*): Originally from Ouarzazate or Spain, the queen of spices is picked with near religious fervor before dawn, which explains its price. Be careful not to buy "counterfeits" for the price of real saffron, sometimes made with silk from corn husks and a little oil! Saffron is used in bourgeois cuisine in the city and in festive dishes.

SAGE (*salmia*): Fresh or dried, sage is used to strengthen tea in winter, and is kneaded into Berber bread dough.

SESAME (*jaljlane*): Sesame is used chopped, ground, or whole and it is a very much sought-after seasoning in Morocco.

TURMERIC (*el kourkoub*): Thank goodness for turmeric! It spares us the use of artificial coloring because it adds its color to simmered dishes naturally. It can replace saffron though sadly it has neither its subtlety nor its strength.

Dried rose buds

Ginger

Ras el hanout

White pepper

Part Three: The Recipes

Recipes for soup, salads, and breads
precede those for main dishes, which begin on page 46

BREADS

Matoula
Country Bread

In the countryside, *matoula* is still cooked in a *ferrah*, an earthenware *tagine* used exclusively for making bread. In the city, an Oujda dish, a cast iron platter, is more common. Oujda dishes can be found in stores run by North Africans.

    5 cups (1 kg) fine wheat semolina
    1 teaspoon salt
    3$^{1}/_{2}$ tablespoons (25 g) yeast or 5 tablespoons
        sourdough starter
    2 cups (500 ml) warm water
    1 cup (200 g) medium wheat semolina

Pour the fine semolina into a large shallow dish. Make a well in the center and add the salt and yeast dissolved in a little of the warm water.

Gradually add the remaining warm water while kneading the dough vigorously. The dough should be softer than regular bread dough. If it is too stiff, add a little more warm water.

Shape the dough into three balls. Sprinkle them with the coarser semolina. Flatten each into a round pancake and place on a clean tea towel, cover completely with another tea towel and allow the dough to rise for 1 hour in a warm place.

Measurements

Measurements in this book are given in volume as far as possible: 1 measuring **cup** contains 250 ml (roughly 8 oz); 1 **teaspoon** contains 5 ml, while 1 **tablespoon** contains 15 ml or the equivalent of 3 teaspoons.

Servings

Unless otherwise stated, all recipes are for 4 to 6 people, as part of a multi-dish meal.

Ingredients

When a recipe lists a hard-to-find or unusual ingredient, see pages 32 and 33 for possible substitutes. If a substitute is not listed, look for the ingredient in a North African or Arabic food market.

Heat the dish or *tagine*. When it's hot, remove the bread from the cloth and cook over low heat, 12 to 15 minutes per side. It must cook slowly, otherwise the crust will burn and the dough inside will remain uncooked. An equally delicious variation is to brush the risen dough with beaten egg yolk and sprinkle with sesame seeds before cooking.

Opposite:
Country Bread (on top), City Bread with Sesame Seeds (in middle), and City Bread (on bottom).

Bride's Fingers

2 tablespoons oil
3 cloves garlic, peeled and crushed with a little
    water to form a paste
1 bunch fresh cilantro (coriander) leaves,
    chopped
$^1/_2$ teaspoon salt
Pinch cumin powder
Juice of $^1/_2$ lemon
1 tomato, peeled, seeded, and finely diced
8 oz (250 g) shrimp (prawns), peeled
1 green chili (optional)
12 sheets *waarka* or filo pastry
1 egg yolk
Oil for deep-frying

Heat 2 tablespoons oil in a pan over high heat and sauté the garlic, cilantro, salt, cumin, and lemon juice. Stir with a wooden spoon for 3 minutes over high heat. Lower the heat, add the tomato and cook for 7 minutes. Add the shrimp and chili (if using) and cook for another 3 to 4 minutes, then remove from heat and cool.

Cut the sheets of *waarka* (or filo) in half. In the middle of each sheet, place 1 tablespoon filling, fold in both sides, then roll to form neat cigar shapes. Seal and brush with egg yolk.

Heat oil in a pan and, when hot, deep-fry the pastries until brown, about 5 minutes. Serve hot.

Crispy Moroccan Crêpes

2 cups (250 g) all-purpose (plain) flour
$^1/_2$ teaspoon salt
1 cup (250 ml) water
5 tablespoons olive oil
1 tablespoon *khli'*, chopped
1 clove garlic

Sift the flour into a mixing bowl with a pinch of the salt. Add water, 2 tablespoons of the oil, and knead until dough becomes elastic. Let the dough rest for 20 minutes.

In the meantime, heat the remaining oil in a saucepan and sauté the *khli'*, crushed garlic, and remaining salt. Simmer 15 minutes.

Divide the dough into approximately ten pieces, each the size of a table tennis ball. Flatten each one on an oiled surface to form a disk. Place 1 teaspoon of filling on each disk. Fold in the sides to form a square. Brush the top with oil and set aside. Heat a pan and brown the squares, 3 minutes each side.

SALADS

Shlada Balfelafla Meshouia
Roasted Bell Pepper Salad

2 green bell peppers (capsicum)
2 red bell peppers (capsicum)
1 tomato, peeled, seeded, and cubed
1 clove garlic
Pinch salt and pepper
Pinch cumin powder
4 tablespoons olive oil

Grill or broil the bell peppers in the oven, approximately 30 minutes, turning regularly, until the skin is completely blistered. Place in a sealed plastic bag or wrap in aluminum foil and allow to cool. When cool enough to handle, peel, remove seeds, and rinse in warm water then pat dry.

Slice peppers into thin strips and arrange on a plate. Add the tomato cubes and sprinkle with chopped garlic. Season with salt, pepper, and a pinch of cumin.

Drizzle with olive oil, then toss and serve warm or cold.

Shlada ba Danjale
Eggplant Salad

2 lb (1 kg) small eggplants (aubergines), stems discarded, sliced lengthways into 4 to 6 pieces
1 small bunch flat-leaf parsley, stems discarded, leaves finely chopped
Large pinch salt
2 tablespoons vinegar
3 tablespoons olive oil
1 teaspoon paprika
1 pinch of cumin powder
3 cloves garlic, peeled and crushed

Blanch eggplants for 10 minutes in salted water.

In a mixing bowl, combine parsley, salt, vinegar, oil, spices, and garlic to form the dressing.

When the eggplant is cooked, drain it, then dip each piece in the sauce and arrange on a serving platter. Serve hot or cold.

Shlada ba Khizou wa Limoune
Carrot Salad with Orange Juice

This recipe is as simple as it is surprising.

  3 medium carrots
  Juice of 1 juicy orange
  1 teaspoon sugar
  $^1\!/_2$ teaspoon cinnamon powder
  1 teaspoon orange flower water
  $3^1\!/_2$ oz (100 g) shelled walnuts

In a mixing bowl, combine the grated carrot, orange juice, sugar, cinnamon, and orange flower water. Mix well. Garnish with the walnuts and serve well chilled.

Zaalouk
Eggplant Purée

  2 lb (1 kg) eggplants (aubergines)
  5 tablespoons olive oil
  2 cloves garlic, peeled and crushed
  1 bunch flat-leaf parsley, leaves finely chopped
  1 bunch fresh cilantro (coriander) leaves, finely chopped
  8 oz (250 g) tomatoes, peeled, seeded, and cubed
  $^1\!/_2$ teaspoon cumin powder
  $^1\!/_2$ teaspoon paprika
  $^1\!/_2$ teaspoon ground black pepper
  1 teaspoon salt
  1 lemon, one half juiced, the other cut in wedges
  12 black olives

Preheat oven to 500°F (250°C, gas 10). Slice the skin of the eggplants lengthwise to prevent them from bursting while cooking. Place them on a baking sheet and bake for 40 minutes, turning occasionally. Allow to cool, then remove the stems and skin. Cut the flesh into cubes and crush with a fork.

Heat the oil in pan and sauté the eggplant, garlic, chopped herbs, tomatoes, spices, salt, and lemon juice. Cook for a further 30 minutes.

Serve hot or cold garnished with the lemon wedges and black olives.

Shlada bal Gharaa
Zucchini Salad

2 lb (1 kg) zucchini (courgettes), stems removed, cut in half then each half quatered lengthways
3 tablespoons olive oil
4 cloves garlic, peeled and crushed
1 bunch flat-leaf parsley, chopped
1 teaspoon salt
1 teaspoon cumin powder
1 teaspoon paprika
Juice of $^1/_2$ lemon

Blanch zucchini in salted water for 5 to 8 minutes. Drain and reserve.

In a pan, heat the olive oil and sauté the garlic, parsley, salt, cumin, and paprika. Stir with a wooden spoon for 3 to 5 minutes. Add the zucchini and stir gently for a further 5 to 7 minutes. Add the lemon juice. This salad may be served hot or cold.

Shlada Bal Foule
Fresh Fava Bean Salad

2 lb (1 kg) fava (broad) beans in the pod, shelled to yield 1 lb (500 g) beans
2 quarts (2 liters) water
2 tablespoons olive oil
1 teaspoon cumin powder
3 cloves garlic, peeled and crushed
1 teaspoon salt
Chili flakes, to taste

Wash the beans and remove the germ but don't peel them. Blanch for 5 to 8 minutes in salted water. Drain and place in a salad bowl.

Add the olive oil, cumin, garlic, salt, and chili and mix thoroughly. Serve hot. You can vary this recipe by mashing the beans with a fork. Also, top with an additional spoonful of olive oil. Delicious!

Shlada B'Khizou Wal Camoune
Carrot and Cumin Salad

4 oz (250 g) medium carrots, peeled, cut in half, each half quatered lengthwise
2 tablespoons olive oil
2 cloves garlic, peeled and crushed
$^1/_2$ bunch flat-leaf parsley, chopped
$^1/_2$ teaspoon ground black pepper
$^1/_2$ teaspoon cumin powder
Juice of $^1/_2$ lemon

Blanch carrot in salted water for 8 to 10 minutes. Drain. Heat oil in a pan and sauté the carrots, garlic, parsley, pepper, and cumin. Just before serving, hot or cold, add the lemon juice. The salad will keep for up to 3 days in the refrigerator.

Limes M'Rakade
Salted Preserved Lemons

2 lb (1 kg) lemons
1 lb (500 g) salt

Clean the lemons thoroughly with a brush under running water. Slice each lemon into quarters without going all the way through the base. Salt them generously, rubbing the salt into the cuts.

Transfer the lemons to a large, sterilized jar, place a weight on top and leave them to marinate 3 days. The lemons should be soaking in their own juices. If here is not enough juice, add a little boiling water to cover the fruit. Seal the jar and set aside for 1 month (away from any source of light or heat). Lemons preserved in this way keep for months.

Matesha M'aasla
Tomato Jam

Rose petals can be found in any Arab grocery.

$^1/_4$ cup (50 g) butter
2 lb (1 kg) very ripe tomatoes, peeled, seeded and diced
1 teaspoon salt
1 teaspoon cinnamon
Pinch of nutmeg
$1^3/_4$ oz (50 g) powdered rose petals
$3^1/_2$ oz (100 g) honey
2 teaspoons confectioners' (icing) sugar
$^1/_3$ cup (50 g) sesame seeds

Melt the butter in a pot, then add the tomatoes, salt, spices, and rose petals. Mix over high heat, then reduce heat and simmer for 40 minutes, stirring from time to time. Add the honey and sugar. Mix well and continue cooking for a further 15 minutes. This jam is delicious on bread (page 35) or plain couscous.

HARIRA BA KAROUIA

Moroccan Caraway Soup

Harira is the star of Ramadan for it is with this soup that the fast is broken.

8 oz (250 g) lamb, cubed small, or chicken livers and gizzards, left whole
1 soup bone, marrow intact
3 onions, peeled and minced
3½ cups (100 g) dry garbanzo beans (chick peas), soaked in cold, salted water the night before, drained
1 heaped tablespoon green lentils
3½ cups (100 g) dried fava (broad) beans, soaked and peeled, drained
1 bunch flat-leaf parsley, chopped
1 small stalk celery
1 tablespoon salt
1 cinnamon stick
1 teaspoon each: ground ginger, black pepper, paprika, cumin, and tumeric
½ cubeb pepper
3 quarts (3 liters) water
1 lb 10 oz (800 g) tomatoes, peeled, seeded and puréed
1 bunch fresh cilantro (coriander) leaves, finely chopped
1 teaspoon caraway seeds

Tadouira

1 cup (125 g) flour
3 cups (750 ml) water
1 teaspoon lemon juice or vinegar

Garnish

2 lemons, cut in wedges
12 dates

Two days before you wish to serve the soup, make the *tadouira* by mixing the flour and water, making sure there are no lumps. Add the lemon juice and rest in a warm place for 48 hours.

In a large *quadra* (see page 29), or in the bottom half of a couscoussier or in a deep stock pot, place the lamb or chicken, the soup bone, onions, garbanzo beans, lentils, fava beans, parsley, celery, and salt.

Add the spices. Cover with the water and bring to a boil. Simmer for at least 1½ hours. The *harira* is not ready until the garbanzo beans lose all of their bite.

When the garbanzo beans are soft, add tomato, cilantro, and caraway. Cook for a further 5 minutes. Remove from heat and stir in the *tadouria*, mixing well with a large wooden spoon. Return to the stove and bring to a boil, then reduce heat and simmer 5 minutes, stirring constantly to prevent it from sticking. Pour into a soup tureen and serve in bowls, with wedges of lemons and dates, which enhance the flavor of this divine soup. A delicious alternative is to add 3½ oz (100 g) cubed *jben* (Moroccan cheese), 2 beaten eggs, and a pinch of salt and pepper after thickening the soup.

MOUROUZIYA

Lamb Confit with Raisins and Almonds

In the past, this *confit* would be kept for months in earthenware jars.

$^{1}/_{2}$ teaspoon salt
1 pinch saffron threads
2 teaspoons *ras el hanout* (see page 33)
4 cups (1 liter) water
6 lamb shanks, or 6 pieces taken from a shoulder of lamb
2 tablespoons peanut oil
2 onions, peeled and thinly sliced
1 tablespoon *smen* (see page 31) or 5 tablespoons salted butter
1 cup (150 g) almonds, blanched and skinned
2 cups (300 g) sultanas or currants
$^{1}/_{2}$ cup (100 g) honey
6 Dadez rose buds, to garnish
$^{1}/_{3}$ cup (50 g) sesame seeds, toasted, to garnish

In a bowl, combine the salt, saffron, *ras el hanout* and 1 cup (250 ml) of the water and mix well. Rub the meat with half of this spice mixture. Reserve the remaining spice mixture for later.

Place the meat in a cast iron pot together with the oil, the remaining 3 cups (750 ml) water, the onions, *smen* (or butter), and almonds. Cook, covered, over low heat for 2 hours. Check the liquid from time to time and add a little water if necessary.

Meanwhile, soak the raisins in warm water. After two hours, drain and add to the meat, along with the reserved spice mixture. Cook a further 20 minutes, then add the honey and continue to cook, uncovered, until the raisins and the almonds start to caramelize.

Serve hot with bread and garnish the dish with rose buds and toasted sesame seeds.

TAGINE BEL GHALMI WAL SFARGEL

Lamb Tagine with Quince

3 lb (1½ kg) shoulder of lamb, cut into
   8–12 pieces
½ cup (100 g) butter
1 stick cinnamon
4 teaspoons ground ginger
3 teaspoons powdered saffron or 10 strands
1 onion, peeled and thinly sliced
½ teaspoon salt
2 lb (1 kg) ripe quinces, halved, cores and
   seeds removed
3 tablespoons honey
1 teaspoon ground cinnamon
1 cup (250 ml) water
1 lb (500 g) okra (ladies' fingers), stems
   removed

In a *tagine* or large pot, combine the meat, butter, cinnamon, ginger, saffron, onion, and salt. Add water to cover the meat, and cook over low heat for 1 hour. When the meat is done, take it out of the pot and reserve it in a covered bowl. Discard the cinnamon stick but retain the pot of liquid.

Place the quinces in the pot of liquid together with the honey, ground cinnamon, and water. Stir gently, bring to a boil and simmer, covered, until the quinces are tender, about 15 minutes.

Return the meat to the pot, along with any juices it releases, then add the okra. Cook for a further 10 minutes. Do not overcook the okra or it will become slimy.

Arrange in a serving dish and serve with bread.

MAQUA BA JEBLANE WA KORNI

Lamb, Pea, and Artichoke Stew

2 lb (1 kg) lamb (preferably from the neck)
2 onions, peeled and sliced thinly
2 cloves garlic, peeled and crushed
2 tablespoons olive oil
1 teaspoon salt
500 ml (2 cups) water
$\frac{1}{2}$ teaspoon paprika
$\frac{1}{4}$ teaspoon ground ginger
$\frac{1}{4}$ teaspoon ground pepper
1 lb (500 g) artichokes (see helpful hint)
1 lemon, one half juiced the other half cut in quarters
3 cups (500 g) fresh shelled peas

In a large pan, place the meat, onions, garlic, oil, and salt. Sauté for 3 to 4 minutes to color the meat evenly. Pour the water over the meat and add the spices. Bring to a boil, then reduce heat and simmer, covered, for 1 hour.

Meanwhile, prepare the artichokes by breaking off the stem and removing the toughest outer leaves. Trim off the top two-thirds, and remove the fuzzy choke, then drop into a mixing bowl filled with water, the juice of half a lemon and the other half cut into quarters. This will prevent the artichokes from discoloring.

After the meat has cooked for 1 hour, add the peas. Five minutes later, add the artichokes. Simmer for a further 15 minutes. If you like your vegetables well done, do not hesitate to leave the pot simmering for another 10 minutes.

To serve, first arrange the meat in a dish, then the artichokes and peas, and finally add the sauce and enjoy it with good Moroccan bread (see page 35).

Helpful hint: Try to look for the small poivrade variety of artichoke. If you use the large globe variety, remove the outer leaves, clean, and quarter them.

TAGINE MAKFOUL

Lamb Tagine with Onions

3 tablespoons olive oil
1 tomato, peeled and sliced
2½ lb (1¼ kg) lamb, neck or shoulder
1 teaspoon salt
3 sticks cinnamon
½ teaspoon saffron threads
½ teaspoon white pepper
2 lb (1 kg) yellow onions (preferably small),
    peeled and sliced into think rings
2 cups (500 ml) water
½ teaspoon ground cinnamon

In a *tagine* or pot (see helpful hint), place the olive oil, tomato, meat, salt, and spices—except the ground cinnamon, which will be used as garnish. Place the onions on top of the meat and add the water. Cover and cook over low heat for 1 hour (1½ hours if you are using a cast iron pot).

Taste and correct the seasoning. Serve directly from the *tagine* if you are using one or arrange the meat on a serving platter. Cover it with the sauce, then garnish with the onions. Sprinkle the whole dish with cinnamon.

Helpful hint: The use of an earthenware *tagine* is recommended for this recipe. If you do not have one, a cast iron pot may be used.

You may substitute red onions that are found throughout the Mediterranean for the small yellow onions if necessary.

KASKSOU TFAYA

Lamb Couscous with Onions

2 lb (1 kg) lamb, neck or shoulder
2 lb (1 kg) onions, peeled and finely chopped
$^1/_2$ teaspoon ground ginger
3 sticks cinnamon
4 cloves
$^1/_2$ teaspoon ground pepper
1 teaspoon salt
1 bunch fresh cilantro (coriander) leaves
1 bunch flat-leaf parsley
6 cups (1$^1/_2$ liters) water
2 lb (1 kg) fine-grain couscous
1 cup (200 g) currants or sultanas
2 tablespoons orange flower water
1 tablespoon *smen* or 5 teaspoons salted butter
1 tablespoon sugar
1 teaspoon ground cinnamon
2 pinches ground saffron
6$^1/_2$ oz (200 g) almonds, peeled, browned in oil
   and chopped
3 hard-boiled eggs, halved, to garnish

In the bottom of a couscoussier, place the meat, onions, ginger, cinnamon sticks, cloves, pepper, salt, cilantro, parsley, and the water. Bring to a boil and simmer for 30 minutes. Taste and correct seasoning as necessary.

In the meantime, prepare the couscous (see page 30 for instructions.)

Soak the currants for about 10 minutes in cold water with 1 tablespoon of the orange flower water.

Remove onions, herbs, and a ladle of stock from the couscoussier. Pour them into a heavy pan with the *smen* (or butter), the sugar, remaining orange flower water and the ground cinnamon and stir until the onions start to caramelize. Add the currants. Simmer for 10 minutes until all the water has evaporated. Discard the herbs.

Form a ring of couscous on a serving platter and place the meat in the middle. Place the currants and the onions on the couscous. Moisten with a little stock. Sprinkle with chopped almonds.

Serve the remaining stock in a tureen and place it in the middle of the table, for guests to serve themselves. You may garnish the dish with hard-boiled egg halves.

TAGINE BAL GHALMI WA ALFOUL

Lamb Tagine with Fava Beans

2½ lb (1¼ kg) shoulder of lamb, cut into
    bite-sized pieces
1 teaspoon salt
½ teaspoon pepper
3 tablespoons olive oil
3 cloves garlic, peeled and crushed with a little
    water to form a paste
2 cups (500 ml) water
½ teaspoon cumin
½ teaspoon paprika
3 lb (1½ kg) fresh fava (broad) beans, or
    2 lb (1 kg) frozen beans, shelled

Season the meat with salt and pepper. Heat oil in a large pot and brown the meat for 5 minutes. Add the garlic, water, and spices. Bring to a boil, then lower heat and simmer for 35 minutes. Add the beans and cook for a further 15 minutes if you like them firm. In Morocco, the beans should be thoroughly cooked, at least 20 minutes or more. Remove from heat.

Arrange the meat on a platter. Add the sauce and, to finish, the beans.

MARQUA BAL KASTEL DIAL TLEMCEN

Tlemcen Chestnut Stew

This recipe originates from Tlemcen, a pretty Algerian town some 50 miles (80 km) from the Moroccan border. If you are using dried chestnuts, you must wash and soak them in cold water the day before you intend to cook. Alternatively, use vacuum-packed or canned chestnuts which do not need to be presoaked and are faster to cook.

3 tablespoons olive oil
2$\frac{1}{2}$ lb (1$\frac{1}{4}$ kg) lamb shoulder, cut into bite-sized pieces
2 onions, peeled and thinly sliced
$\frac{1}{2}$ teaspoon salt
$\frac{1}{4}$ teaspoon saffron threads
$\frac{1}{4}$ teaspoon ground nutmeg
1 stick cinnamon, broken in two
1 cup (250 ml) water
13 oz (400 g) dried chestnuts, or 1 lb (500 g) vacuum-packed or canned chestnuts
1 tablespoon sugar
1 tablespoon orange flower water

In a large pot, heat the oil, then add the meat and brown for a minute or two. Add the onions, salt, spices, and water, then stir, and bring to a boil.

If using presoaked, dried chestnuts, add to the pan, reduce heat and simmer 45 minutes. If using vacuum-packed or canned chestnuts, allow the meat to cook for 30 minutes before adding the chestnuts. Check from time to time and add an extra $\frac{1}{2}$ cup (125 ml) water if the sauce has evaporated. Check for doneness: the chestnuts should be soft and the meat tender.

Next add the sugar and the orange flower water. Reduce the sauce over low heat until it thickens.

Arrange the meat in a serving dish, cover with the chestnuts, and pour over the sauce.

TAGINE BAL GHALMI WA GHARAA WA NA'NA'

Lamb Tagine with Zucchini and Mint

2 tablespoons olive oil
2 lb (1 kg) lamb shoulder, cut into 6 pieces
1 stick cinnamon
Large pinch saffron threads
$1/4$ teaspoon ground pepper
$1/2$ teaspoon salt
3 cloves garlic, peeled and crushed
2 cups (500 ml) water
Oil for deep frying
2 lb (1 kg) zucchini (courgettes), tips
    removed, washed and dried then
    thinly sliced
$1/2$ teaspoon salt
Pinch ground pepper
1 sprig mint leaves, washed and chopped (keep
    a few leaves whole and garnish)

Heat the oil in a large pot and add the meat, cinnamon stick, saffron, pepper, salt, and garlic. Mix and brown the meat evenly. Pour the water around the meat (not directly over it). Bring to a boil, then lower the heat and simmer for 45 minutes. Taste and correct seasoning if necessary.

Heat the oil for deep-frying in a pan and deep-fry the zucchini, then remove with a slotted spoon and reserve.

Arrange the meat in a serving dish with the slices of zucchini on top. Add salt, pepper, and chopped mint leaves. Garnish with whole mint leaves and serve.

DAL'AA M'AMRA B'KASKSOU WATMAR

Shoulder of Lamb with Couscous and Date Stuffing

1 teaspoon salt
1 shoulder of lamb, about 3 lb (1½ kg),
    boned and butterflied ready for stuffing
¼ teaspoon saffron threads
½ teaspoon pepper
1 tablespoon butter
1 tablespoon *smen*, or 5 tablespoons salted
    butter

Stuffing
  ½ cup (100 g) raisins
  1 tablespoon orange flower water
  8 oz (250 g) cooked couscous
  ½ cup (100 g) butter, melted
  ½ cup (100 g) sugar
  1 teaspoon ground cinnamon
  ¾ cup (100 g) almonds, peeled and chopped
  1 cup (150 g) dates, pits (stones) removed,
    diced

Garnish
  6–8 almonds, peeled and toasted
  6–8 dates, pits (stones) removed

Rub the salt into the meat and steam in the top of a couscoussier for 1 hour, checking regularly that the water has not boiled off.

To prepare the stuffing, soak the raisins in water with ½ tablespoon of the orange flower water for 15 minutes. Then combine the couscous (see page 32), melted butter, soaked raisins, sugar, cinnamon, chopped almonds, dates, and the remaining orange flower water. Set aside.

In a bowl, mix the saffron, pepper, butter, and *smen*. Remove the meat from the steamer and coat it with the prepared saffron-butter mix. Stuff the lamb with the stuffing and, using a needle and strong cooking thread, sew the opening shut. Roast for 30 minutes in an oven preheated to 250°F (180°C, gas 4).

While the meat is roasting, prepare the garnish by stuffing each date with a toasted almond.

Place the roast on a serving platter, then cut the thread to allow the stuffing to spill out. Garnish the meat with the stuffed dates.

Helpful hint: Use a colored thread to sew the meat so it is easier to locate when carving.

TAGINE BEL GHALMI WAL BARKOUK WA GELJLANE

Lamb Tagine with Prunes and Sesame Seeds

3 lb (1$\frac{1}{2}$ kg) shoulder or neck of lamb,
    cut into 6–8 pieces
5 tablespoons olive oil
1 stick cinnamon
3 teaspoons ground saffron or 10 saffron
    threads
$\frac{1}{2}$ teaspoon ground black pepper
2 onions, peeled and thinly sliced
1 teaspoon salt
11$\frac{1}{2}$ oz (350 g) prunes
$\frac{1}{2}$ cup (100 g) sugar
1 teaspoon ground cinnamon
$\frac{1}{2}$ cup (100 g) butter
$\frac{1}{2}$ cup (125 ml) water

Garnish
1$\frac{1}{4}$ cups (150 g) almonds, peeled and
    toasted (see page 40)
Handful toasted sesame seeds

Place meat in a large pot with oil, cinnamon stick, saffron, pepper, and onions. Add salt, cover with water, bring to a boil, and simmer 1 hour.

When the meat is done, remove it from the pot and keep covered. Discard the cinnamon stick.

Add the prunes, sugar, ground cinnamon, and butter to the pot. Stir in the $\frac{1}{2}$ cup water, mix and simmer, covered, until the sauce thickens to a syrupy consistency.

Return the meat to the pot along with any juice it has released and simmer for a further 15 minutes.

Serve the meat in a large dish with the sauce and prunes, and garnish with toasted sesame seeds and a sprinkling of almonds.

MECHOUI

Spit-roasted Lamb

There are numerous ways to prepare a *mechoui*. Townsfolk in Morocco generally take the meat to the local baker to be cooked in his bread oven but traditionally it is roasted on a spit in the open air. A large hole is dug in the ground 1½ yards (1½ m) long, 2 feet (60 cm) wide, and 1½ feet (50 cm) deep. A wooden fire is lit in the hole and the cooks wait for embers to form. The whole lamb is threaded onto a spit and balanced on forked poles that have been placed on either side of the pit. The lamb is then cooked for about 6 hours during which time it is basted from time to time with melted, salted butter.

For those unsure about digging up their garden, *mechoui* can be rotisserie grilled above a large barbecue grill or roasted in a conventional oven.

1 young milk-fed lamb, 15–20 lb (8–10 kg) for rotisserie grilling above a barbecue grill, or 1 leg or shoulder of lamb for roasting
1½ cups (300 g) butter, melted and mixed with 1 tablespoon salt

Condiments

2 tablespoons salt
2 tablespoons ground pepper
2 tablespoons cumin powder

If using a large barbecue grill, light the charcoal (arrange the coals in two piles at each end so they are below the shoulder and thighs) and run the turnspit through the lamb, starting from the rear. Insert the two-pronged skewers at each end to hold the lamb in place and use wire to fasten the lamb to the turnspit if necessary. Rub the lamb with the salted butter, then attach the turnspit to the rotisserie Baste it with the remaining salted butter every 30 minutes. After about 2 hours rake some of the coals to the center of the pit for cooking the belly of the lamb. After about 3 to 3½ hours check for doneness. The meat is done when the outside is dark brown and crispy, the meat is beginning to split, and the internal temperature is about 170°F (80°C). Remove the lamb from above the fire and rest for 15 minutes before taking out the turnspit.

If using a conventional oven, cook the basted leg or shoulder at 500°F (250°C, gas 10) for 30 mins then reduce heat to 300°F (150°C, gas 2) and continue to cook, basting occasionally, until the lamb is done (about 25 mins per ½ lb/1 kg.)

Fill three small bowls with salt, pepper, and cumin. Place the lamb on a large serving platter, and serve it accompanied with the condiments. A *mechoui* can be served with eggplant, zucchini, and bell pepper salads (see pages 40 to 42). Serves 12.

TAGINE KEFTA BAL BEID

Meatball Tagine with Eggs

5 cups (800 g) ground veal (or any cut of beef for mincing)

1 large onion, peeled and finely chopped

1 bunch fresh cilantro (coriander) leaves, chopped

1 teaspoon salt

$1/2$ teaspoon ground pepper

1 teaspoon paprika

5 tablespoons olive or ·peanut oil

2 large tomatoes, peeled, seeded, and roughly chopped

6 eggs

In a mixing bowl, combine the veal, onion, chopped cilantro, salt, pepper, and paprika. Rinse your hands in cold water, then shape the balls by rolling the mixture between the palms of your hands. Moisten your hands between rolling each meatball.

Heat the oil in a tagine or other earthenware dish and sauté the meatballs over medium-high heat for 15 minutes. Halfway through cooking the meatballs, add the tomato and mix well.

Break the eggs over the meatballs as you would for fried eggs. Cover the tagine and cook for a further 3 minutes. Serve hot. Delicious!

Helpful hint: To peel tomatoes, score the base crosswise, then transfer to a pan (off the heat). Pour boiling water over the tomatoes and leave for 1 minute. Drain and, when cool, slip off the skins.

MARQUA BAL LA'GEL WA CHIFLORE

Veal Stew with Cauliflower

Water to boil cauliflower
2 teaspoons salt
1 head firm cauliflower, broken into florets
3 tablespoons olive oil
2¹/₂ lb (1¹/₄ kg) stewing veal
1 onion, peeled and thinly sliced
2 teaspoons pepper
¹/₂ teaspoon saffron threads
2 bay leaves
2 cups (500 ml) water
6 eggs
2 cloves garlic, peeled and crushed
3 tablespoons all-purpose (plain) flour
Oil for deep-frying

Bring a pot of water with 1 teaspoon of the salt added to a boil. Add the cauliflower, cook for 15 minutes (or less, to taste), then drain.

In a large pot, place 3 tablespoons olive oil, the veal, onion, remaining salt, 1 teaspoon of pepper, saffron, bay leaves, and 2 cups (500 ml) water. Bring to a boil over high heat, taste, correct seasoning, and cover. Reduce heat and simmer for 45 minutes.

Meanwhile, break the eggs into a mixing bowl and beat. Add the remaining pepper, mix, add the garlic, mix again, and set aside. Put the flour on a plate and set aside.

Heat the oil in a frying pan. Take a cauliflower floret, dip first in egg, then in flour, then fry in oil, ensuring that each piece is evenly browned, about 5 to 7 minutes. Drain on paper towels. Cook all the cauliflower in this way, adding more flour if necessary. Remove the veal from the heat. Transfer it to a serving dish and arrange the cauliflower on top.

MARQUA BAL BARANIA

Foreigners' Chicken and Eggplant Stew

I was born in a border town where "immigration" was a common word. Recipes also emigrate, settle, and move on, sometimes departing unchanged, sometimes altered, on their way to more distant horizons. This is one such recipe that was just passing through.

- 1 onion, peeled and thinly sliced
- 1 free-range chicken, cut into 6 pieces
- 1 cup (250 ml) water
- 1 garlic bulb, left whole
- 3 tablespoons olive oil
- 1 teaspoon salt
- 1 teaspoon ground black pepper
- 1 teaspoon ground cinnamon
- 1 teaspoon paprika
- 1 bunch flat leaf parsley, chopped
- 1 bunch fresh cilantro (coriander) leaves, chopped
- Oil for deep-frying
- 2 lb (1 kg) eggplant (aubergines), sliced $3/4$ in (2 cm) thick, wiped clean

Garnish

- 1 preserved lemon, chopped (see page 43)

In a large pot, put the onion, chicken, water, whole head of garlic, oil, salt, spices, and herbs. Bring to a boil, then lower heat, and simmer, covered, for 45 minutes.

Heat the oil for deep-frying in a pan and deep-fry the eggplant slices, then remove with a slottde spoon and drain on paper towels. Slice the eggplant into thin strips.

Arrange the chicken on a platter, make a little nest of eggplant on each piece of chicken, then garnish with chopped preserved lemon.

TAGINE BAL GHAMI WA KARMOUSSE

Chicken Tagine with Figs

`Chicken

2 tablespoons olive oil
1 free-range chicken, cut into 8 pieces
2 onions, peeled and sliced
2 cloves garlic, peeled and crushed
$^1/_2$ teaspoon ground ginger
$^1/_2$ teaspoon salt
Several saffron threads
1 bunch fresh cilantro (coriander) leaves,
   chopped
1 cup (250 ml) water
5 tablespoons butter
1 tablespoon honey
5 tablespoons butter or *smen* (see page 31)

Figs

1 teaspoon ground cinnamon
$^1/_2$ teaspoon ground ginger
$^1/_2$ teaspoon nutmeg
$^1/_2$ teaspoon ground pepper
$^1/_2$ teaspoon salt
1 tablespoon water
2 lb (1 kg) fresh figs

Garnish

$6^1/_2$ oz (200 g) shelled and halved walnuts

To prepare the figs, in a mixing bowl, combine the spices, salt, and water. Add the figs, toss gently, and marinate for 1 hour.

Meanwhile, in a cast iron pot, place the oil, chicken, onions, garlic, ginger, salt, saffron, and cilantro. Add the water, bring to a boil, then reduce heat and simmer for 45 minutes, stirring from time to time.

Prepare two skillets. Melt 5 tablespoons butter in one. Drain the figs, place in the pan with the honey and cook gently for 7 minutes.

In the other pan, melt the remaining 5 tablespoons butter or *smen*. Drain chicken and brown each piece.

When all the chicken has been browned, arrange the pieces on a platter and pour the warm cooking juices over the chicken. Garnish with the figs and sprinkle with walnut halves.

DJAJE BA ṢANOUJ

Nigella Seed Chicken

1 free-range chicken
2 heaped teaspoons nigella seeds, 1 teaspoonful
    crushed and the other left whole
6 tablespoons olive oil
2 onions, peeled and cut in thin slices
Pinch of ground ginger
1 teaspoon salt
Pinch of pepper
2 cups (500 ml) water
Several saffron threads
1 bunch fresh cilantro (coriander) leaves
1 large or 2 small preserved lemons (see
    page 43), quartered

Rub the chicken with the 1 teaspoon of crushed nigella seeds and place in a pot. Add the olive oil, onions, ginger, salt, and pepper. Over high heat, brown the chicken evenly, about 5 minutes. Add the water and saffron. Bring to a boil. Add the cilantro, the whole nigella seeds, and preserved lemon. Cover and simmer for 40 minutes.

Transfer the chicken to a serving dish and pour the sauce from the pot over it, ensuring that it is covered with seeds and lemon pieces. Serve hot.

TAGINE DJAJE BA ZITOUNE WA L'HAMED

Chicken Tagine with Olives and Preserved Lemons

1 free-range chicken
4 tablespoons olive or peanut oil
$\frac{1}{2}$ teaspoon salt
Pinch of ground pepper
Pinch of ground ginger
Pinch of saffron threads
1 stick cinnamon or $\frac{1}{2}$ teaspoon ground
   cinnamon
1 onion, peeled and thinly sliced
1 tomato, peeled, seeded and chopped
1 bunch flat-leaf parsley, chopped
1 bunch fresh cilantro (coriander) leaves,
   chopped
4 cloves garlic, whole
2 cups (500 ml) water
$6\frac{1}{2}$ oz (200 g) olives, preferably purple
1 preserved lemon (see page 43)

In a heavy pot, brown the chicken in oil with the salt, spices, and onion, for 7 minutes, stirring the meat to color evenly. Add the tomato, herbs, and whole garlic cloves. Add the water, bring to a boil, lower heat, and simmer for 45 minutes.

When the meat is cooked, take a ladle of stock from the pot and heat it in a small saucepan with the olives and lemons. Reduce stock for at least five minutes.

When serving, arrange the chicken in a *tagine*, cover with sauce, olives, and lemons. Serve bread as an accompaniment (see page 35).

TAGINE BA DJAJE WA MACHMACHE WA LOUZ

Chicken Tagine with Dried Apricots and Pine Nuts

Chicken

- 1 free-range chicken, cut into 6 pieces
- 4 tablespoons peanut oil
- 1 teaspoon salt
- $^1/_2$ teaspoon ground pepper
- $^1/_4$ teaspoon ground ginger
- Pinch of saffron threads
- 1 stick cinnamon
- 2 small onions, peeled and thinly sliced
- 1 cup (250 ml) water
- $3^1/_2$ oz (100 g) pine nuts, toasted in a dry pan (do not burn)

Apricots

- 1 lb (500 g) dried apricots, rinsed
- 1 cup (250 ml) water
- $^1/_2$ cup (100 g) sugar
- 1 teaspoon cinnamon
- $^1/_2$ cup (100 g) butter

To prepare the apricots, place them in a saucepan with water, sugar, cinnamon, and butter. Bring to a boil. Cook over low heat, uncovered, until the liquid has reduced to a syrupy consistency.

In a large pot, brown the pieces of chicken in hot oil. Season with salt, pepper, ginger, saffron, and cinnamon stick. Add the onions and water. Simmer for 30 minutes, covered over low heat. When the chicken is done, arrange the pieces of meat with the sauce on a serving platter. Garnish with apricots and pine nuts.

DJAJE MFEWAR

Stuffed Steamed Chicken

1 free-range chicken
$^1/_2$ teaspoon salt
2 quarts (2 liters) water
2 bay leaves
3 carrots, peeled
3 onions, peeled
6 potatoes, peeled
1 bunch fresh cilantro (coriander) leaves
1 bunch flat-leaf parsley

Stuffing

1 bunch fresh cilantro (coriander) leaves,
  finely chopped
1 bunch flat-leaf parsley, finely chopped
4 cloves garlic, peeled and crushed
1 onion, peeled and thinly sliced
1 teaspoon salt
1 teaspoon ground pepper
1 teaspoon cumin powder
1 teaspoon paprika

Accompaniments

1 teaspoon cumin
1 teaspoon salt

To prepare the stuffing, combine all the stuffing ingredients and mix well. Set aside.

Rub the skin of the chicken with salt, fill with the stuffing and sew the opening shut using a large needle and thread.

In the bottom of a couscoussier, heat the water with the bay leaves. In the basket of the couscoussier, place the chicken, the whole vegetables, and the herbs. Cover with aluminum foil and cook for 1 hour over simmering water.

Discard the herbs. Halve the carrots lengthways and cut the onions and potatos into bite-sized pieces. Serve hot in a large dish with the chicken in the middle and the vegetables in a ring around it. Accompany with two saucers of cumin and salt.

Helpful hint: Use a colored thread to sew up the birds, so it will be easier to locate when carving.

L'HMAME MAARAR B'KASKSOU

Couscous-stuffed Pigeon

²/₃ cup (100 g) dark raisins
2 cups (500 ml) water
1 tablespoon orange flower water
1¼ cups (250 g) fine-grain couscous
5 tablespoons *smen* or salted butter
³/₄ cup (100 g) almonds, blanched and peeled,
   sautéed in oil until golden, chopped
Pinch of nutmeg
½ teaspoon saffron
1 tablespoon honey
6 pigeons, cleaned and prepared by the
   butcher
2 onions, peeled and cut in thick slices
3 tablespoons olive oil
1 teaspoon salt
½ teaspoon white pepper
½ teaspoon ground ginger
3 cloves
2 cinnamon sticks
2 cups (500 g) water

Soak the dark raisins in 2 cups (500 ml) of water and 1 tablespoon of orange flower water for 1 hour. Drain well.

Prepare the couscous according to the instructions on page 30. Place it in a large mixing bowl. Add the *smen* or butter, chopped almonds, drained raisins, nutmeg, saffron, and honey. Mix well. Stuff the pigeons with half of the mixture and sew them shut using a large needle and thread.

Place the onions in a large pot with 3 tablespoons olive oil. Place the pigeons on top. Season with salt and pepper and the remaining spices and add 2 cups (500 ml) water. Cover and continue cooking over high heat for a few minutes. Taste and correct seasoning. Lower the heat and cook for 1 hour. Check the sauce and add an additional ½ cup (125 ml) water, if needed. Meanwhile, heat the reserved couscous.

Arrange the pigeon on a dish, remove the string and serve with the additional couscous.

B'STILLA BAL HMAME

Moroccan Pigeon Pie

3 tablespoons olive oil
4 large onions, peeled and sliced
2 bunches fresh cilantro (coriander) leaves, chopped
4 bunches flat leaf parsley, chopped
1 teaspoon *ras el hanout* (see page 34)
6 tender young pigeons, plucked and cleaned
1 cup (250 ml) water
10 eggs, beaten

Almond paste

3 cups (400 g) almonds, with their skins
2 tablespoons oil for frying
$^1/_2$ cup (100 g) sugar
$^1/_2$ teaspoon ground cinnamon
1 tablespoon orange flower water

Pastry

30 sheets *waarka* (see page 31) or filo pastry
$^3/_4$ cup (150 g) melted butter
2 egg yolks

Garnish

$^3/_4$ cup (100 g) confectioners' (icing) sugar
1 teaspoon ground cinnamon

In a large pot, mix the olive oil, onions, herbs, and the *ras el hanout*. Add the pigeons and sauté over high heat. Add the water and bring to a boil then cover, reduce heat and continue cooking for 45 minutes. Remove the pigeons and reduce sauce over low-medium heat for another 20 minutes. While the sauce is cooking, debone the pigeons. After 20 minutes is up, add the beaten egg to the sauce, whisking constantly. Remove from heat as soon as the sauce begins to thicken (do not scramble).

To make the almond paste, blanch and peel the almonds, then cook in oil until golden; be careful not to burn them. Put through the food processor until finely ground. In a bowl, mix ground almond with the sugar, cinnamon, and orange flower water. Stir or knead until mixture forms a thick paste.

Butter a pan, 15 in (35 cm) in diameter, and layer 4 sheets of *waarka*, each brushed with butter, on the base. Fan additional sheets out from the center (two-thirds of the sheet extending beyond the rim of the pan) and brush each sheet with butter. Layer half the almond paste over the base, cover with the egg mixture, then a layer of pigeon meat, and finally the remaining almond paste. Close the seams by folding the overhanging pastry towards the center and seal with egg yolk.

Bake for 20 minutes at 400°F (200°C, gas 6). Unmold onto a serving dish and decorate with confectioners' sugar and cinnamon.

Helpful hint: If you are unable to find pigeon, make the same pie using one whole chicken instead of the six pigeons.

B'STILLA BAL HOUTE

Moroccan Seafood Pie

1 quart (1 liter) mussels, washed
3 tablespoons olive oil
3 cloves garlic, peeled and crushed
2 plump tomatoes, peeled and diced
1 onion, peeled and cut into thick slices
1 lemon, cut in half, one half juiced and the
    other half diced (with peel on)
1 teaspoon salt
$\frac{1}{2}$ teaspoon ground pepper
$\frac{1}{2}$ teaspoon ground paprika
$\frac{1}{2}$ teaspoon ground cumin
10 oz (300 g) mushrooms, wiped clean
    and sliced
2 carrots, grated
$6\frac{1}{2}$ oz (200 g) squid, cut in strips
$6\frac{1}{2}$ oz (200 g) European pollack (pollock) or
    other cod-like fish, cut in large chunks
$11\frac{1}{2}$ oz (350 g) medium shrimps (prawns),
    washed
1 cup (200 g) butter
20 sheets *waarka* or filo pastry
2 bunches fresh cilantro (coriander) leaves,
    chopped
2 bunches flat-leaf parsley, chopped
1 egg yolk
6 black olives
Lemon slices to garnish

Place the mussels in a large pot, cover, and cook for 7 to 9 minutes over high heat. The mussels should open. Remove the meat and discard the shells, as well as any unopened mussels. Set aside in a mixing bowl.

In the same pot, heat the oil and add the garlic, tomatoes, onion, lemon juice, diced lemon, salt, pepper, paprika, cumin, mushrooms, and grated carrots. Cook over medium-high heat, covered, 5 to 8 minutes.

Add the squid and continue to cook for 10 minutes; add the fish and shrimps and cook a further 10 minutes. Turn off the heat and remove the shrimps. Set aside about 18 shrimps for garnish, two-thirds of them peeled, the rest left unpeeled. Peel the remaining shrimps and return to the pot.

Brush the butter on one side of each sheet of *waarka* (or filo). Butter a 15-in (35-cm) baking pan. In the middle of the pan, place 4 sheets of pastry, overlapping. Arrange another 8 sheets in a ring extending out over the edge of the pan. Fill the pan half-full with the seafood mixture, drained of its sauce. Fold the overhanging leaves towards the middle, and cover with a second layer of filling. Cover with the remaining sheets and form a seam with the pastry over the edges. Seal with egg yolk. Bake for 20 minutes at 400°F (200°C, gas 6). Unmold onto a serving dish and garnish with shrimps (unpeeled and peeled), olives, and lemon slices.

TAGINE BAL HOUT

Fish Tagine

In Morocco, we enjoy eating shad and pandora fish. Allis shad is often difficult to find and caution should be exercised when eating it because of its many bones. To make this tagine, you can use European pollack (pollock) instead of the pandora fish.

    3 tablespoons olive oil
    3 lb (1$^1/_2$ kg) European pollack (pollock), pan-
        dora, or any cod-like fish, cut into
        6$^1/_2$ -oz (200-g) pieces
    3 plump tomatoes, peeled and cut in rings
    1 green bell pepper (capsicum), cut in rings
    3 cloves garlic, peeled and crushed
    1 preserved lemon, cut in wedges (see page 43;
        you can also substitute $^1/_2$ of a fresh lemon,
        but the taste will be different)
    6$^1/_2$ oz (200 g) olives
    $^1/_2$ teaspoon ground pepper
    $^1/_2$ teaspoon ground cumin
    2 cups (500 ml) water
    1 bunch flat-leaf parsley, chopped
    1 bunch fresh cilantro (coriander) leaves,
        chopped

In an eathernware *tagine* or large, cast-iron pan, heat the oil and add the pieces of fish, tomato, green bell pepper, garlic, preserved lemon cut into wedges (or half fresh lemon), olives, pepper, cumin, and water. Simmer for 35 minutes if using a pot, 45 minutes if using a *tagine*.

Serve in the *tagine* or arrange the fish in a dish, garnished with the tomato, pepper, olives, lemon, parsley, and cilantro.

SARDINE MAAMRINE

Stuffed Sardines

Allow three sardines per person and try to find the smaller, less oily, Mediterranean sardines.

2 lb (1 kg) sardines, boned and cut in half lengthways by the fishmonger
2 tablespoons olive oil
$\frac{1}{2}$ lemon, thinly sliced
$\frac{1}{2}$ teaspoon salt
$\frac{1}{2}$ teaspoon ground turmeric
$\frac{1}{2}$ teaspoon ground cumin
$\frac{1}{4}$ teaspoon ground white pepper
2 plump tomatoes, peeled, seeded, and chopped
2 cloves garlic, peeled and crushed
4 tablespoons water
$3\frac{1}{2}$ cup (100 g) olives

Stuffing

1 bunch fresh cilantro (coriander) leaves, chopped
1 bunch flat-leaf parsley, chopped
2 cloves garlic, peeled and crushed
Juice of $\frac{1}{2}$ lemon
1 tablespoon rice
$\frac{1}{2}$ teaspoon salt
$\frac{1}{2}$ teaspoon ground turmeric
$\frac{1}{2}$ teaspoon ground cumin
$\frac{1}{4}$ teaspoon ground white pepper
2 tablespoons olive oil

To prepare the stuffing, combine the cilantro, parsley, garlic, lemon juice, rice, salt, turmeric, cumin, pepper, and oil. Mix well and set aside.

Place half a sardine on a plate, cover with a tablespoon of stuffing, then cover with the second fillet. Stuff all the sardines the same way.

On a baking tray, spread the oil, lemon slices, salt, the spices, tomatoes, and garlic. You may also add any leftover stuffing. Arrange the sardines neatly over this mixture and add 4 tablespoons of water. Bake at 400 to 425°F (200 to 220°C, gas 6 to 7), for 20 minutes.

Serve on a platter with the baked lemons and olives.

KASKOU BEL HOUT

Fish Couscous

3 tablespoons oil
2 onions, peeled and sliced
2 cloves garlic, peeled and crushed
2 small whole eggplants (aubergines)
3 carrots, peeled and cut in half
3 turnips, peeled and cut in half
1 lb (500 g) squash (marrow), peeled and cut in half
2 tomatoes, peeled and diced
$\frac{1}{2}$ lemon
1 teaspoon cumin
1 bunch fresh cilantro (coriander) leaves
4 cups (1 liter) lightly salted water
3 good-sized sea bream, scaled, gutted, and rinsed clean
6 pieces European pollack (pollock) or sea bass
Pinch salt
5 cups (1 kg) fine-grain couscous
$\frac{1}{2}$ teaspoon ground saffron

In a pot, place the oil, onions, garlic, and vegetables. Add lemon, cumin, cilantro, and 4 cups (1 liter) salted water. Cover and cook over medium heat for 25 minutes. Drop the fish into the stock, cook for 10 minutes, then remove. Bring the stock back to a boil, add the salt, and discard the cilantro.

While the vegetables are cooking, make the couscous as instructed on page 30, adding the saffron to color and flavor the grains.

Serve the couscous in a dish with the fish in the middle, surrounded by the vegetables. Ladle a little stock over the dish and serve extra stock on the side.

L'HOUT BA LOUZ WA TMARE

Rock Cod with Almonds and Dates

3 lb (1½ kg) rock cod or scorpion fish
Juice of ½ lemon
1 teaspoon salt

Stuffing

10 oz (300 g) whole dates, pitted to yield
    6½ oz (200 g) pitted dates
1¼ cups (150 g) almonds, blanched and
    peeled, sautéed in oil until golden
2 large onions, peeled and chopped, sauteed in
    2 tablespoons oil over low heat
½ teaspoon ground nutmeg
½ teaspoon ground saffron
Pinch of salt
½ teaspoon ground black pepper
5 tablespoons *smen* or salted butter
1 tablespoon orange flower water
4 tablespoons oil

Scale, gut, and wash the fish, remove the central bone but leave the head on and the fillets attached (or have your fishmonger do this). Rub the skin with juice from half a lemon and 1 teaspoon salt. Set aside.

To prepare the stuffing, grind dates and almonds together in food processor. Prepare the fried onion. Combine the minced dates and almonds, onions, spices, salt, pepper, *smen*, orange flower water and a few more drops of lemon juice, then mix well. Fill the fish two-thirds full, then sew shut.

Preheat the oven to 425°F (220°C, gas 7). Oil a baking dish and add the fish. Form any additional stuffing into little balls and place around the fish. Bake for about 30 minutes or until done. Serve in a dish surrounded by the little balls of stuffing as garnish.

BTATA B'FLIOU

Wild Thyme Potatoes

This simple dish is surprisingly tasty and can be prepared very quickly.

1 bunch wild thyme
3 tablespoons olive oil
1 onion, peeled and thinly sliced
1 teaspoon salt
Pinch of white pepper
1 cup (250 ml) water
3 lb (1½ kg) new potatoes (alternatively use roseval or any other firm, waxy variety)
2 plump tomatoes, peeled and sliced

Quickly rinse the thyme, reserve a few whole sprigs for the garnish, and remove the flowers and leaves from the other sprigs.

In a large pot, preferably cast iron, heat the oil and sauté the onion for 5 to 7 minutes until golden. Add salt, pepper, and water and bring to a boil. Add the potatoes and tomatoes, cover, reduce heat, and cook for 10 minutes. Add the thyme leaves and flowers, cover again, and cook for a further 15 minutes. Taste and correct seasoning, if necessary.

Transfer to a serving dish. The potatoes should be cooked through, but firm. Add the sauce and garnish with the reserved thyme.

KASKOU LAKDAR

"Green" Couscous

1 lb (500 g) zucchini (courgettes), blossoms
   attached if possible
1 onion, peeled and quartered
1 teaspoon salt
$\frac{1}{2}$ teaspoon white pepper
$\frac{1}{2}$ teaspoon ground ginger
$\frac{1}{4}$ teaspoon saffron threads
Harissa or other chili paste (see page 32)
1 bunch fresh cilantro (coriander) leaves
6 cups (1$\frac{1}{2}$ liters) water
3 tablespoons olive oil
11$\frac{1}{2}$ oz (350 g) fresh fava (broad) beans
   (or 3$\frac{1}{2}$ oz/200 g frozen), shelled
8 oz (250 g) fresh peas (or 5 oz/150 g frozen),
   shelled
5 cups (1 kg) medium-grain couscous

Wash the zucchini, reserve six for the garnish, and cut the others in quarters.

In a large pot, place the onion, salt, spices, cilantro, and water. Bring to a boil, taste and correct the seasoning. And the oil, beans, peas, and zucchini. Cook for 20 minutes over low heat.

Meanwhile, cook the couscous according to the instructions on page 30. Serve in large, shallow dish, preferably in earthenware. Make a dome of couscous. Flatten the top of the dome and place the vegetables in the middle. Pour the stock over the vegetables.

Helpful hint: Connoisseurs should use fine couscous. If you enjoy spicy food, omit the harissa and serve with fresh green or red chilies. Harissa is a mixture of chilies and spices that can overpower the subtle flavors of this vegetable couscous.

BISSARA DAL FOUL LYABESS

Fava Bean Purée

Bissara is a pauper's dish that has become the food of kings. It is succulent and can be served as a first course or as a soup with the evening meal.

  2 tablespoons olive oil
  1 lb (500 g) dried fava (broad) beans
  6 cloves garlic, peeled and crushed
  1 teaspoon ground cumin
  1 teaspoon ground paprika
  2 teaspoons salt
  2 quarts (2 liters) water

Garnish
  1 teaspoon ground cumin
  1 teaspoon ground paprika
  1 tablespoon olive oil

In a large pot, heat the oil and cook the beans, uncovered, over medium heat with the garlic, cumin, paprika, salt, and water. Stir from time to time.

When the beans are very well cooked, about 1 hour, put through a food mill, then reheat for a few minutes. Pour into a shallow dish.

Enjoy your *bissara* hot or cold, with a sprinkling of cumin, paprika, and a drizzle of olive oil.

Wheat Pudding

8 oz (250 g) whole-grain wheat, soaked in
   2 cups (500 ml) water with 1½ teaspoons
   salt for 1 hour
2 cups (500 ml) water
½ teaspoon salt
4 cups (1 liter) milk
1 tablespoon superfine (caster) sugar
1 tablespoon orange flower water

Garnish

4 tablespoons honey

Drain the wheat, then bring to a boil in 2 cups (500 ml) water with ½ teaspoon salt, and simmer for 35 minutes. Drain again.

Bring the milk to a boil and add the wheat, sugar, and orange flower water. Simmer for an additional 10 minutes. Serve hot like a soup with honey on top.

MHANCHA

The Snake

Almond paste

1 lb (500 g) almonds, blanched and peeled
$^2/_3$ cup (150 g) superfine (caster) sugar
1 teaspoon ground cinnamon
2 tablespoons orange flower water
3/4 cup (150 g) butter, softened

Pastry

20 sheets *waarka* or filo pastry
1 egg white
$^1/_2$ cup (100 g) butter
$3^1/_2$ oz (200 g) honey

Prepare the almond paste by putting the almonds and the sugar through a food mill (or a food processor). Add the cinnamon, orange flower water, and soft butter. Mix until the paste holds its shape in a ball. Then roll the paste into long snake-like rolls. Set aside.

On your work surface, place the sheets of *waarka* in a long row, slightly overlapping. Seal the seams between the sheets with slightly beaten egg white.

Preheat oven to 400°F (200°C, gas 6).

Line up the snakes of almond paste along the length of the pastry, then roll the paste in the pastry. Carefully coil the snake into a spiral.

Tranfer the snake to a buttered, round baking dish. To make the pastry crisp, evenly distribute little pieces of butter over the surface of the pastry. Bake 10 minutes until golden.

Remove from oven and cover with slightly warmed honey. Cool before serving.

SEFFA

Cinnamon Rice Pudding

2¾ cups (600 g) short-grain (pudding) rice
1 tablespoon oil
2 cups (500 ml) milk
¾ cup (150 g) butter
1 teaspoon ground cinnamon
2 teaspoons confectioners' (icing) sugar
3½ oz (100 g) almonds, blanched and peeled
Oil for deep-frying

In a mixing boil, coat the rice evenly with the oil. Steam in the upper half of a couscoussier for 10 minutes above boiling water.

Rinse the rice in cold water and return to the mixing bowl. Sprinkle with a little milk, and steam for another 10 minutes. Repeat the process 7 times.

The seventh time you steam the rice, fold in the butter, separating the grains of rice.

On a serving dish, make a dome with the rice. Starting from the top, draw lines of sugar and cinnamon on the rice. Garnish with almonds and serve hot.

KNAFFA

Layered Custard Stacks & Layered Milk Stacks

LAYERED CUSTARD STACKS

4 cups (1 liter) milk
$1\frac{1}{4}$ cups (200 g) superfine (caster) sugar
2 eggs, beaten
3 tablespoons orange flower (or rose) water
12 sheets *waarka* or filo pastry
5 tablespoons butter
10 dates
18 shelled walnut halves

To make the custard, bring the milk just to boiling point in a saucepan, add the sugar and mix well. Remove from heat and add the eggs one at a time, whisking thoroughly. Return to heat, stirring constantly. Bring to a boil, remove from heat and add the orange or rose water, then leave to cool.

Paste two sheets of *waarka* together with a little butter. This will make the layers more stable when assembling. In a frying pan over low heat, toast until golden in a little more butter. Cook all the pastry in pairs in the same manner.

When ready to serve, alternate layers of pastry with the custard. Decorate with dates and walnuts.

LAYERED MILK STACKS

1 lb (500 g) almonds, with their skins
2 tablespoons peanut oil
$\frac{2}{3}$ cup (150 g) superfine (caster) sugar
12 sheets *waarka* or filo pastry
5 tablespoons butter
2 cups (500 ml) milk
$\frac{1}{2}$ tablespoon orange flower water

Nowadays, you will find that this recipe often replaces the one for layered custard stacks, as it is easier to prepare.

Blanch and peel the almonds, then fry in the oil, drain on paper towels, and chop. Add the sugar to the almonds and mix. Set aside.

Prepare the *waarka* as in the recipe for layered custard stacks.

On a serving platter, place the first pair of *waarka* sheets and sprinkle with almond/sugar mixture. Continue stacking, alternating layers, and finish with a layer of pastry. Just before serving, pour warm milk flavored with orange flower water over the dish.

BARWAT BA LOUZ, CIGARS BA LOUZ

Almond Triangles & Almond Cigars

ALMOND TRIANGLES

Almond paste

4 cups (500 g) almonds, blanched, peeled, and finely ground
2/3 cup (150 g) superfine (caster) sugar
1 teaspoon ground cinnamon
2 tablespoons orange flower water

Pastry

20 sheets *waarka* or filo pastry
Oil for deep-frying
Honey

Mix the finely ground almonds with the sugar, cinnamon, and orange flower water until you form a thick paste.

Cut the sheets of pastry into 4 strips, place a spoonful of filling at one end, fold over the corner to make a triangle, then continue folding at right angles. To seal, tuck in the opposite end like an envelope (see page 31).

Fry the triangles in hot oil until golden. Drain on paper towels. Roll each pastry in a dish of melted honey and serve on an attractive platter.

ALMOND CIGARS

Almond paste

1 1/2 cups (200 g) almonds, blanched and peeled
3 1/3 tablespoons (100 g) superfine (caster) sugar
1 teaspoon ground cinnamon
1/3 cup + 2 teaspoons (100 ml) orange flower water

Pastry

12 sheets *waarka* or filo pastry
Oil for deep-frying
1 egg, beaten
Honey

In a food processor, grind the almonds to a fine powder.

Mix the powder with the sugar, cinnamon, and orange flower water. Knead into a ball. Separate into small pieces and roll each piece into a stick 2 1/2 to 3 in (6 to 7 cm) long.

Cut the sheets of *waarka* into rectangles, place a stick along one short edge, fold in the two sides, then roll up like a cigar. Seal with beaten egg.

Fry the cigars in hot oil. Drain on paper towels, then roll each cigar in a dish of melted honey. Arrange on a platter and serve cold.

KAAB EL GHOZAL

Gazelle Horns

These cakes are sometimes called "gazelle horns" in English, but why that is remains a mystery. In Arabic, *kaab el ghozal* means "gazelle ankles!" This recipe makes 60 to 70 horns.

Almond paste
8 cups (1 kg) blanched and peeled almonds
2 cups (500 g) superfine (caster) sugar
2 tablespoons orange flower water
1 tablespoon melted butter

Dough
1 tablespoon melted butter
4$\frac{1}{2}$ cups (500 g) all-purpose (plain) flour
$\frac{1}{3}$ cup + 2 teaspoons (100 ml) orange flower water

Mix the almonds and the sugar, grind in a food mill or a food processor and reduce to a fine powder. Mix this powder with the orange flower water and the melted butter. Separate the mixture into pieces the size of a walnut and roll into batons about 1 x $\frac{1}{3}$ in (3 x 1 cm). Set aside.

Mix all the ingredients for the dough together until firm. Roll the dough as thin as possible with a rolling pin. It should be almost transparent. Place the baton of almond paste on the dough in a line with even spaces between each baton. Fold the dough over to cover all the pieces of almond paste. Seal by pressing slightly and separate with a pastry cutter. Bend each piece slightly to form a crescent.

Prick each biscuit with a pin to allow the steam to escape during baking. Transfer to a baking sheet, brush with melted butter, then bake for approximately 10 minutes at 400°F (200°C, gas 6). The horns should be barely golden.

You can serve them plain or dusted with confectioners' (icing) sugar.

Helpful hint: For less experienced pastry chefs, you can replace the dough with 1$\frac{1}{2}$ cups (200 g) toasted sesame seeds. Beat two eggs in a bowl, dip the sticks of almond paste first in the egg, then in the seeds, shape into crescents, and bake for 7 minutes at 400°F (200°C, gas 6).

ASSIR LOUZ

Traditional Almond Milk & Enriched Almond Milk

TRADITIONAL ALMOND MILK

4³/₄ cups (600 g) almonds
4 cups (1 liter) water
1 cup (250 g) superfine (caster) sugar
1 teaspoon orange flower water (optional)

Fill a large saucepan with water. Bring to a boil. Add the almonds and cook 5 minutes. Drain the almonds, rub them in your hand to remove skins, then wipe dry. Pound into a smooth paste.

In a food processor, place the almonds, water, and sugar, and mix thoroughly. Add orange flower water and serve very cold.

ENRICHED ALMOND MILK

4³/₄ cups (600 g) almonds
4 cups (1 liter) low-fat (semi-skim) milk
1¹/₄ cups (300 g) superfine (caster) sugar
1 teaspoon orange flower water (optional)

Prepare as for the previous recipe but instead of water, use milk. It is richer, but it is very good!

ATAI BA NA'NA

Green Mint Tea

4 cups (1 liter) water
1 teaspoon Gunpowder tea, or other Chinese
    green tea
4–6 lumps of sugar
1 bunch fresh mint

Start by boiling the water. Put the tea in a small teapot. Add 1 or 2 glasses of boiling water, then discard the water, making sure to leave the tea leaves in the pot. Wash and pat dry the mint and add to the teapot. Of course, the more mint you use, the more fragrant the tea will be. Fill the teapot with boiling water, not simmering water as you would for black tea.

Add the sugar. Close the lid and pour out a glass of tea. Pour the contents of the glass back into the teapot and repeat 3 or 4 times until the ingredients are completely mixed. Serve.

Index